GENDER AND THE CONSTRUCTION OF DOMINANT, HEGEMONIC, AND OPPOSITIONAL FEMININITIES

GENDER AND THE CONSTRUCTION OF DOMINANT, HEGEMONIC, AND OPPOSITIONAL FEMININITIES

Justin Charlebois

LEXINGTON BOOKS
a Division of
ROWMAN & LITTLEFIELD PUBLISHERS, INC.
Lanham • Boulder • New York • Toronto • Plymouth, UK

Published by Lexington Books
A division of Rowman & Littlefield Publishers, Inc.
A wholly owned subsidiary of The Rowman & Littlefield Publishing Group, Inc.
4501 Forbes Boulevard, Suite 200, Lanham, Maryland 20706
www.lexingtonbooks.com

Estover Road, Plymouth PL6 7PY, United Kingdom

British Library Cataloguing in Publication Information Available

Library of Congress Cataloging-in-Publication Data

Charlebois, Justin, 1978–
  Gender and the construction of dominant, hegemonic, and oppositional femininities / Justin Charlebois.
    p. cm.
  Includes bibliographical references and index.
  ISBN 978-0-7391-4488-6 (cloth : alk. paper) — ISBN 978-0-7391-4490-9 (electronic)
  1. Femininity. 2. Sex role. I. Title.
  BF175.5.F45C45 2011
  305.42—dc22   2010037758

Contents

Acknowledgments

I am particularly indebted to Raewny Connell, James Messerschmidt, and Mimi Schippers for developing the theoretical constructs that underpinned the research presented in this book. I would like to extend special appreciation to James Messerschmidt for reading the entire manuscript and providing invaluable feedback.

I would also like to extend my appreciation to Lexington Books for making this project possible. I am especially grateful to Michael Sisskin for expressing interest in my work and seeing this book through to completion.

Finally, I would like to thank my family. A special thanks to my mother, Patricia, for being a continual voice of encouragement and steadfast supporter. I am also blessed to have Kate as my sister, a trusted friend, supporter, and compassionate human being. Finally, gratitude to my father, John, for providing me with the precious gifts of wonderful memories of summers spent in northern California as well as insightful advice and encouragement.

Introduction

The twenty-first century is supposedly a post-feminist age where gender equality is a given and fundamental human right. Women are ostensibly guaranteed equal access to school athletics, employment opportunities, and assured of the same opportunities as men. Nevertheless, equality opportunities rhetoric sharply contrasts with the disparities that women face. Connell (2009, 132) succinctly points out that women's incomes are slightly more than half of men's, necessitating financial dependence on a male breadwinner. Women not only face a significant wage gap, but also unequal access to senior positions with authority in government, corporations, and religious organizations (Connell 2009, 120). As of this moment, while progress toward a goal of gender equality has been made, the march toward gender equality is far from over.

Socially constructed notions of masculinity and femininity or social actions and behaviors that we attribute to and thus associate with men and women can arguably both empower and disempower individuals. For example, the strong association between masculinity and corporate management may result in an unfair situation where a male applicant receives an automatic advantage over a female one. In this case, notions of masculinity and femininity advantage men but disadvantage women. Unfortunately, as leadership is commonly gendered masculine, men may also be promoted to administrative positions in stereotypically feminine professions such as nursing and paralegal work. To take another example, since medicine is typically considered masculine, women may face obstacles as they attempt to demonstrate their professional competence. This example illustrates the much more disturbing phenomenon that masculinity is superior to femininity. While men's entry into feminized professions actually increases the occupations' social prestige, the feminization of certain occupations is negatively viewed. Significantly, a fundamental disparity exists where men are sometimes welcomed into stereotypically feminine professions, but women are discouraged from entering masculine ones due to femininity's contaminating effect on these professions.

The focus of this book is on socially constructed notions of femininity and how those norms can impact women's choices and behaviors. Specifically, I investigate current conceptualizations of dominant, hegemonic, subordinate, and oppositional femininities. It is an overstatement to claim that socially constructed notions of femininity are the single obstacle which prevents the attainment of true gender equality. Nevertheless, I would argue that dominant notions of femininity and the pressure to conform to those norms can exert a degree of influence on women's behaviors and consequently their choices. For instance, essentialist ideas of female sexuality construct women as relationship-oriented and unable to separate sexual activity from emotional attachment (Hamilton and Armstrong 2009, 593). I would argue that an orientation toward heterosexual monogamy is merely a socially constructed norm constituting heterosexual femininity and women and men have equal capacity for sexual promiscuity. Therefore, some men are emotionally driven and sexually monogamous while some women are sexually promiscuous. However, men and women are judged differently for engaging in similar activities because a social imperative sanctions permissive male sexuality and stigmatizes nonmonogamous female sexuality. As a result, irrespective of personal desires, women may conform to this social norm to avoid cultural marginalization.

Overview of the Book

The first chapter provides an overview of some of the book's foundational terms such as sex, gender, and accountability. Drawing on West and Zimmerman's (1987) seminal concept of *doing gender*, I argue that gender is not a fixed trait residing within individuals, but a social construct that is fluid, variable, and situated in specific social contexts. Nonetheless, individuals are held accountable to socially constructed notions of masculinity and femininity. By aligning their actions with or against socially sanctioned notions of gender-appropriate behavior, individuals sustain or subvert notions of gender. Gender subversion, however, rarely goes unnoticed and is frequently punished, thus individuals may find it more comfortable to align their actions with dominant notions of masculinity and femininity. This chapter also includes a discussion of social structure to illustrate how macro-level processes can inhibit individual gender accomplishments. The final section of the chapter considers the notion of *crisis tendencies,* which posits that social changes can disrupt the stability of gender relations.

Chapter 2 continues a discussion of key terms concerning masculinity and femininity. The main focus of the chapter is a discussion of dominant, hegemonic, subordinate, and oppositional femininities. I provide a thorough discussion of these key concepts which are the theoretical constructs I utilize for the later empirical analysis chapters. In the final section of the chapter, I provisionally identify some characteristics constituting white, middle-class, dominant femininity in the United States.

The next chapters use dominant, hegemonic, subordinate, and oppositional femininities as theoretical constructs to empirically investigate the construction of gender in schools, workplaces, and media. Chapter 3 illustrates how heterosexuality is still a regulatory force on adolescent female sexuality and a definitive component of both dominant and hegemonic femininities. A girl's school-based popularity is not entirely determined by her heterosexual desirability, but forming a romantic relationship with a high-status boy greatly enhances her popularity. Disturbingly, this example also illustrates how a girl's popularity is at least partly contingent upon securing a heterosexual relationship, where boys evaluate their heterosexual desirability, while a boy's popularity derives from scholastic and athletic achievements, which are based on individual merit, not obtaining others' recognition and approval. The chapter also considers two case studies of oppositional femininities who challenge and subvert normative notions of heterofemininity and the consequences of their gender transgression.

The focus of chapter 4 is on the social construction of gender in the workplace. The chapter begins with a discussion of the relationship between a long-standing gender division of labor and its relationship to notions of masculinity and femininity. The latter section of the chapter explores how professional women construct their gendered professional identities in the nontraditional occupations of police work, law, corporate management, and the priesthood. A noteworthy finding is that women face a perennial double bind between constructing a professional identity and their feminine accountability. As masculine characteristics are often the sine qua non of professional success, women can inadvertently subvert notions of femininity in the process of professional identity construction. However, women who conform to notions of femininity can engender critical judgment as ineffective or unsuccessful professionals. In order to resolve this double bind, professional women devise a number of unique strategies which enable them to simultaneously co-construct their gender and professional identities.

Chapter 5 shifts the focus of the book from individuals' construction of gender within key social institutions to media representations of gender. Nonetheless, I argue that the media does not simply represent but actively constructs gender. With this in mind, I analyze media constructions of gender in several key media programs. I initially focus my analysis on several immensely popular Disney films produced during the latter part of the twentieth century. Disturbingly, in spite of portraying somewhat self-confident protagonists, these films draw on the seemingly timeless fairy-tale narrative which portrays women as inherently incomplete and unfulfilled until they enter long-term heterosexual relationships. Disappointingly, their accomplishments are undermined by a ubiquitous quest for heterosexual romance. In the second part of the chapter, I specifically focus on single women by analyzing gendered representations in *Fatal Attraction, Bridget Jones's Diary,* and *Sex and the City.* Significantly, these media texts both subvert and reify aspects of dominant femininity. These media celebrate single life as a temporary state but ultimately sustain the desirability and normativity of long-term heterosexual relationships. Similar to Disney, women are constructed as incomplete without a romantic heterosexual relationship.

Finally, the concluding chapter draws together the book's main findings and arguments, and discusses oppositional femininities' crucial role as potential catalysts for equalizing gender relations.

The next chapter forms the book's foundation by discussing the active process of constructing gender.

1

The Social Construction of Gender

Recently, gender is conceptualized neither as something individuals are born with nor acquire solely through socialization, but as an active accomplishment that is done differently within specific social and cultural contexts (Connell 2009; Messerschmidt 2004; West and Fenstermaker 1995; West and Zimmerman 1987). Despite the dynamic nature of gender construction, individuals are not entirely unconstrained to freely do gender, but their agency is somewhat curtailed by social institutions which prescribe situationally appropriate accomplishments of gender. In this chapter, I adopt a social constructionist perspective of gender which integrates my dual concerns of social structure and individual agency and serves as the theoretical framework of this book (Connell 2009; Messerschmidt 2004; West and Fenstermaker 1995; West and Zimmerman 1987).

Doing Gender, Doing Difference

Individuals in many Anglophone societies assume that others are neatly classifiable into one of two sex categories, male or female, based upon the possession of genitalia or chromosomal typing (West and Zimmerman 1987, 127). This dichotomy is maintained in social interaction through a process known as sex attribution or assigning individuals sex category membership based upon socially agreed-upon criteria which constitute masculinity or femininity such as physical appearance, behavior, and dress (West and Fenstermaker

1995, 20). To illustrate, we might conclude on the basis of a muscular build, deep voice, and three-piece suit that an individual possesses male sex category incumbency. Biological sex does not determine, but usually influences, the sex category membership that others ascribe to us. A notable case where biological sex and sex category membership do not concur is that of the transsexual *Agnes* (Garfinkel 1967).

Agnes possessed the biological criteria of a penis and consequently was raised as a boy; however, she adopted the self-attribution of a female and eventually underwent sex reassignment surgery. Agnes apparently bought into the essentialist notion of bifurcated sex categories and consequently attempted to pass as a female prior to surgery. Agnes not only adopted a feminine style of dress but also behavior such as not displaying assertiveness and successfully claimed female category incumbency (West and Zimmerman 1987, 134). Notably, the possession of a penis was unrelated to Agnes's ability to act and be recognized by others as a woman. West and Zimmerman (1987) importantly point out that genitalia are conventionally hidden from view, so they are not the main criteria from which individuals determine sex category membership. Nonetheless, individuals do not question the veracity of the existence of dichotomous sex categories but instead accept this as commonsense and consequently ascribe others to one of two categories. Presumably, Agnes also accepted the naturalness of dichotomous sex categories and thus attempted and successfully claimed female category membership prior to sex reassignment surgery. Importantly, Agnes contributed to our understanding of how biological sex and sex category membership can misalign and that gender or "normative conceptions of attitudes and activities appropriate for one's sex category" (West and Zimmerman 1987, 127) is actively accomplished in specific social settings.

Significantly, Agnes transformed our notions about the naturalness of unequivocal sex categories and illustrated how claiming category incumbency is a social and interactional accomplishment. Therefore, physical behavior, style of dress, and manner of speaking are all part of a repertoire of social actions that together constitute masculinity and femininity and notably vary by society, social situation, and change over time. Despite the fluidity of gender, individuals typically configure and orchestrate their social actions in accordance with socially sanctioned notions of masculinity and femininity.

West and Zimmerman (1987, 135–36) draw on the notion of accountability to reflect how individuals design and self-regulate their actions in light of how others might view and characterize those actions. Individuals are typically accountable to gendered actions and behaviors deemed normative according to ascribed sex category membership. Since Agnes was seen as possessing female category incumbency, she was held accountable to feminine actions and behaviors such as style of dress, manner of speech, and displaying unassertiveness, which enabled her to successfully *do* femininity. Agnes chose to align her social actions with those rendered acceptable for female sex category membership despite the possession of male genitalia; however, individuals possess agency to accomplish gender in multifarious ways. For example, a transgendered individual or *transgenderist* may not wish to pass as a member of either sex but instead construct an androgynous gender identity (Bolin 1994, 479). Therefore, the active process of *doing gender* does not mean that sex category membership determines gendered behavior, but that individuals "*engage in behavior at the risk of gender assessment*" (West and Zimmerman 1987, 136). For example, a man possesses agency to publicly display emotion or vulnerability in North America; however, these feminine social actions may incur a negative assessment from others which could materialize in the form of a derogatory epithet such as *fag* (Pascoe 2007) or even physical violence (Connell 1995, 80). Similarly, a transgenderist's decision not to claim male or female sex category membership may result in social stigmatization and incur sanctions. Conceivably, if more men engaged in feminine behaviors such as crying or expressing vulnerability, they would no longer stand out as remarkable and instead become part of a repertoire of masculine social actions. However, clearly demarcated masculine and feminine social actions are crucial to the process of doing gender, so it is unlikely that society will exhibit greater tolerance for feminized men or transgenderists in North American societies. It is more likely that these individuals will need to account for their subversive behavior and currently accepted ways of doing gender and resulting institutional arrangements will remain intact (West and Zimmerman 1987, 146).

A fundamental and enduring assumption of dimorphic sex-based categories means that creating and reifying sex-based differences is one way to do gender (West and Zimmerman 1987, 137). Gender differences can be accentuated or minimized through dress (single-sex versus unisex clothing), physical size (muscular versus slim build), and physical adornment such as makeup, jewelry, and accessories. As Connell (2009, 53) perspicuously points out, reproductive difference is assumed to impact a range of other areas such as physical skills (men have mechanical ability while women are good at detailed work), character (men are aggressive while women are nurturing), and intellect (men are rational, women have intuition). Notably, the salience of these gender differences can be manipulated to serve patriarchal ends. The employment patterns of women further demonstrates this point. During times of war, governments have deemphasized women's domestic role and encouraged them to enter the paid labor force to fill a labor shortage (Weedon 1987, 125). Women were later encouraged to reenter the home following men's return from combat. Significantly, gender differences can be emphasized or overlooked to exclude women from aspects of public life and reify a patriarchal gender order.

As I have discussed, gender attribution is a social process where bifurcated gender categories are created and sustained. Transgendered individuals represent a third gender category which indicates that dimorphic gender categories created on the basis of assumed biological sex are a culturally constructed, not natural phenomenon. Some Native American Indian societies even distinguish a third gender: *berdache* (Roscoe 1998). These examples nicely illustrate how biological sex is not necessarily a template for gender.

A ubiquitous assumption of binary differences seems to drive much social interaction and structures unequal institutional arrangements. For example, some women may *opt out* (Stone 2008) of professional employment not because of a purported maternal instinct but due to their partner's minimal contribution to domestic labor and childcare. Therefore, an essentialist assumption that women have a predisposition for mothering results in the formation of unequal gender relations within the family, workplace, and in society. An exclusive focus on gender differences both overemphasizes and distorts sexual differences and diverts attention away from sex-based similarities and differences among men and women. Significantly, the overall finding from a century of sex difference research is that men and women are psychologically very similar (Connell 1987, 170; Connell 2009, 62). This means there is no empirical basis for claims espousing sex-based differences in brain anatomy and functioning, mathematical ability, or verbal ability (Connell 2009, 52, 66). There is nothing in the genetic makeup of women which prevents them from becoming scientists or men from becoming primary school teachers. Although the popular press claims that men and women can be likened to different species who often miscommunicate (Gray 1992; Tannen 1990), empirical research dispels these myths. As Deborah Cameron (2007, 181) eloquently states, "Men are from Earth. Women are from Earth."

We also need to acknowledge that men and women are not homogenous categories; therefore, intra-group variation exists according to age, socioeconomic class, race, sexuality, and individual variation. For instance, a reductionist claim, such as *men are stronger than women*, ignores both same-sex differences and the fact that some women are stronger than some men (Connell 1987, 80). These differences can also become more or less salient within particular social milieux such as schools, families, and workplaces. A focus simply on gender differences ignores other factors such as race, social class, and sexuality which intersect and inform the social accomplishment of gender.

The active accomplishment of gender intersects and thus operates concomitantly with social class and race; hence, Fenstermaker and West (1995) claim that gender is not only done differently in specific social contexts but also accomplished differently in conjunction with social class and race. So while a middle-class woman may elect to opt out (Stone 2008) of the paid workforce and become a full-time mother, this choice is contingent upon and reflective of both her social class and marital status and would not be an option for a single mother or married woman of another social class. This is just one example of a class-specific form of femininity but nonetheless illustrative of the point that gender and social class can and do intersect.

The significance of the simultaneous doing of gender, race, and social class is that institutional inequalities are attributable to natural differences between groups of people (Fenstermaker and West 2002, 207). Doing gender, race, or class differently is not problematic in and of itself; however, and significantly, the oppressive nature of gender stems from the inferences and consequences of those differences (West and Zimmerman 2009, 117). An assumption of natural differences and subsequent allocation of job duties based upon sex category membership can contribute to the formation of a *patriarchal dividend* (Connell 2009, 142) where men accumulate material wealth and social power from maintaining a patriarchal gender order.

Doing gender, doing difference remains a powerful intellectual tool to conceptualize gender as a situated, active accomplishment. In their recent clarification of the concept, West and Zimmerman (2009, 118) acknowledge that an investigation of the body's role in maintaining or subverting sex category incumbency can only "complicate and deepen our understanding of doing gender." The work of Messerschmidt (2000, 2004) builds on and extends doing gender by explicitly foregrounding the body's role in the active production of gender.

Gender as an Embodied Interactional Accomplishment

Messerschmidt (2000, 2004) also views gender as accomplished through individuals' self-regulated actions; however, normative conceptions of masculinity and femininity can curtail or structure individual action. As discussed, sex category membership renders individuals accountable to masculine or feminine social actions; therefore, most of us configure and orchestrate our actions in line with normative gendered expectations, lest we face stigmatization. Accordingly, the doing of gender is somewhat curtailed or structured by these normative expectations and needs to be conceptualized as *embodied structured action* or "what people, and therefore their bodies, do under specific social structural constraints" (Messerschmidt 2004, 40). Social structures refer to "regular and patterned forms of interaction over time that constrain and channel behavior in specific ways" (Messerschmidt 2004, 39). Therefore, individuals accomplish gender through the embodiment of gender appropriate or inappropriate social actions and in the process reify or potentially challenge current social structures. Macro-level social structures such as divisions of labor, relations of power, and sexuality and micro-level, face-to-face accomplishments of gender mutually influence one another in a dialectical fashion. Significantly, social structures simultaneously constrain and enable particular gendered social actions which in turn reify or transform those structures (Messerschmidt 2004, 40).

The lived body is the key site where gender differences are constructed and thus gender (masculinities and femininities) is accomplished. Accordingly, bodily similarities between men and women are disregarded while differences are exaggerated (Messerschmidt 2004, 49). For instance, women's purported physical and emotional weakness or can be invoked in order to justify their exclusion from military academies or the armed forces. Kimmel (2000) nicely points out how military service is seen as gender conforming for men but nonconforming for women; therefore, men view women as a threat to their "pristine homosocial institution" (502). This example further illustrates how bodily differences can be strategically manipulated to justify and maintain unequal gender relations.

Messerschmidt's (2004) life-history interviews with violent adolescent offenders offer profound insight into the multifarious ways lived bodies constrain and enable our capacity to accomplish gender. For example, Kelly apparently rejected nearly all aspects of femininity from an early age and instead adopted a fundamentally masculine *gender project* (Connell 1995, 72). Kelly was close to her stepfather and together they engaged in the masculine embodied social actions of building furniture, watching sports, and working on automobiles (Messerschmidt 2004, 94–95). Unlike the *women* of the household, Kelly and her stepfather were permitted to eat in front of the television, make a mess, and were exempt from participation in domestic labor. Although Kelly's biological sex and embodied gendered behavior were incongruent, her stepfather encouraged her masculine behavior and therefore her masculine embodiment was neither remarkable nor deviant within the home.

In the social milieu of the school, Kelly initially self-identified as a member of the jock group, but she was eventually rejected by this group because she wore "boys' clothes" and was labeled a *dyke* by the other girls (Messerschmidt 2004, 97). Unfortunately, Kelly was also rejected by the jock boys, who called her a "wimp" and told her to "stop acting like a guy." Kelly experienced a conflict at school because she was seen as possessing female sex category membership, which did not concur with her masculine embodied social actions, thus others negatively assessed her accomplishment of gender. Despite

Kelly's embodiment of masculinity her physical body prevented her from violently responding to these insults, which illustrates how the body can inhibit our accomplishment of gender.

Kelly was troubled by the continual abuse of her male peers and turned to her stepfather for advice (Messerschmidt 2004, 98). Unsurprisingly, her stepfather encouraged Kelly to respond to their taunts with verbal threats and physical violence. Play fighting became another masculine social action which Kelly and her stepfather engaged in and became a turning point for Kelly's place within the school. Through the experience with her stepfather, Kelly no longer accepted verbal abuse from her male peers but instead physically responded to their insults (Messerschmidt 2004, 99). Kelly was careful to only fight with boys whom she could physically overtake but nevertheless adopted a tough attitude. Although Kelly was never accepted by the jocks, she was able to gain some masculine confidence and respect through participation in assaultive violence.

In the eighth grade, Kelly began to hang out on the street with the badass guys, a group of boys who frequently caused troubled in school and engaged in crime outside of school (Messerschmidt 2004, 100). Similar to Kelly, these boys adopted a tough guy attitude and accordingly "did not take shit from anyone." Significantly, Kelly was the only girl who hung with the badass boys, and she expressed distaste toward the permissive sexuality displayed by the badass girls. Kelly gained honorary guy status and was uninterested in engaging in sexual relations with the badass boys, although she self-identified as heterosexual.

Kelly's token male status afforded her with the privilege of engaging in masculine embodied social actions with the badass boys. Whereas the badass girls only fought with other girls, Kelly fought exclusively with boys, which raised her status in the group. Kelly played video games with the guys, went driving with them, and engaged in fighting with other street groups. Like her home, Kelly was able to embody masculinity within the social milieu of the street.

Despite Kelly's honorary male status with the badass boys, her female sex category membership ultimately resulted in her preclusion from certain activities and subordination within the group (Messerschmidt 2004, 101). Although Kelly participated in physical fights with the other boys, she was excluded from engaging in burglaries and robberies because the boys were afraid she would get hurt. Kelly's exclusion from participation in crime indicates that she was ultimately accountable to her female sex category membership despite displaying masculine embodied social actions and that females occupied a subordinate position within this group.

Kelly's life-history interview indicates the constraints imposed by the physical body on our ability to embody masculinity or femininity. Kelly's physical body initially inhibited her from physically responding to verbal assaults at school. Presumably, physically weak boys who are the targets of verbal and physical abuse experience a similar dilemma. Through the assistance of her stepfather, Kelly was able to eventually transform her physical body into a resource which enabled her to respond to verbal threats with physical violence. Kelly's body became a weapon which enabled her to gain membership into the badass group and become *one of the guys* (Miller 2001). However, Kelly's female body ultimately inhibited her from attaining full guy membership as she was prevented from participating in organized crime. Significantly, the male group members attached social significance to Kelly's biological sex in order to subordinate her and maintain male power. There was nothing in Kelly's life-history interview which indicates that she was physically weaker than the other boys; however, they utilized the popular stereotype of *weak woman* to oppress Kelly.

Kelly's life-history interview is further evidence that gender differences are far from natural, but socially constructed and manipulated to sustain patriarchal power. Kelly was awarded honorary, albeit partial, male status and thus able to participate in a range of masculine embodied social actions along with the boys; however, and significantly, they used her *weak female body* as the basis for her exclusion from participation in burglaries and robberies. Conceivably, these harder forms of crime distinguished the *men* from the *boys* and thus were a key resource for demonstrating one's masculinity and ultimately a source of power. Since the boys were unwilling to share this power with a female, the stereotype of a weak female body was used to disempower Kelly and highlights how natural differences can be invoked to maintain patriarchal power (Weedon 1987, 2) and ensure that women do not benefit from the patriarchal dividend (Connell 2009, 142).

Unequal gender relations are normative in many gangs and materialize in the form of male leadership, a double standard with regard to sexual activities, the sexual exploitation of some young women, and deliberate exclusion of most young women from serious gang crime (Miller 2001, 181). Although Kelly was able to engage in some masculine embodied social actions, the boys, who not coincidentally wielded power in the group, decided that she was ultimately accountable to female sex category and thus femininity. Significantly, there was no basis for their decision to exclude Kelly from participation in hard crime. Quite conceivably, Kelly was physically capable of engaging in more serious forms of crime along with the boys; however, to do so would have challenged and potentially undermined the disparate gender relations in the group and ultimately masculine power. Therefore, natural differences were invoked to discipline Kelly and thus illustrates that gender differences can be made salient by those in power to rationalize and maintain unequal gender relations.

Gender Relations

The discussion thus far has illustrated that while gender is actively accomplished on a moment-to-moment basis within specific social mileux, sex-category membership renders individuals accountable to masculinity and femininity. As a result, agency is somewhat curtailed in that individuals tend to align their social actions with socially sanctioned notions of masculinity and femininity. Agency is not only curtailed by notions of masculinity and femininity but also by social structures. According to Connell (1987), "the concept of social structure expresses the constraints that lie in a given form of social organization" (93). Connell uses this definition of social structure as the basis for her *gender relations approach* (1987, 1995, 2009), which provides us with a model that incorporates the notion of multiple masculinities and femininities and at the same time acknowledges the structural constraints on gender (Connell 1987, 1995, 2009). According to Connell (2009), "when we look at a set of gender arrangements, whether the gender regime of an institution or the gender order of a whole society, we are basically looking at a set of *relationships—* ways that people, groups, and organizations are connected and divided" (73). Connell draws on West and Zimmerman's (1987) concept of doing gender and locates the formation of relationships between men and women and among men or women in face-to-face interactions that are located within specific social institutions. Relations between masculinity and femininity and among masculinities or femininities can be found within power relations, production relations, emotional relations, and symbolic relations (Connell 1987, 2009).

Power Relations

The influential work of Michael Foucault (1977) has demonstrated that power is not simply unidirectional and oppressive but omnidirectional and therefore can also be empowering. Women's liberation movements exemplify how existing forms of knowledge which position men in positions of relative power in relation to women can be challenged and repressed groups can attempt to disrupt patriarchal gender relations. Nevertheless, masculinity usually occupies a dominant position over femininity and thus a patriarchal structure of gender relations is normative in many social institutions.

Connell acknowledges that power is fluid and thus individuals shift between positions with relative degrees of power. Therefore, men exercise power over women through overrepresentation in key positions within workplace organizations and an unequal division of domestic labor and material wealth (Connell 1987, 107).

Power also operates more insidiously through discourses or "practices that systematically form the objects of which they speak" (Foucault 1972, 49). More concretely, discourses are "forms of knowledge or powerful sets of assumptions, expectations and explanations, governing mainstream social and cultural practices" (Baxter 2003, 7). For example, a *gender differences* discourse (Sunderland 2004) positions men and women as naturally suited to perform different social tasks due to biologically based differences. Women's childbearing capacity predisposes them not only for childcare but also for certain pastoral professions such as nursing and elementary school teaching. Men, on the other hand, are naturally aggressive and thus suited for careers in management or politics. An issue with this discourse is that it exaggerates and distorts the significance of women's reproductive capacity by extending it to the social realm and it fails to account for why masculine is more highly valued than feminine (Connell 2009, 58). Surely men and women both have the capacity to care (Connell 2000, 191; Messerschmidt 2000, 141) and inflict damage on children, as cases of child abuse or abandonment indicate. This discourse is particularly damaging to women because it constructs femininity not simply as different from but subordinate to masculinity. It is no mistake that masculine characteristics such as aggressive competitiveness are idealized in the public realm of work and feminine characteristics are conveniently *disappeared* (Fletcher 1999). As my discussion of women working in nontraditional occupations will indicate, women's success in certain professions is contingent upon their adopting particular masculine characteristics and de-emphasizing feminine ones. Power relations are also intricately linked to the type of labor men and women perform or production relations.

Production Relations

The gender division of labor forms the basis for many of our assumptions about gender. In modern western societies, a common division of labor is between work and home (Connell 2009, 79). Work is done outside the home and incurs wages, a symbol that an individual has produced something worthwhile and has thus positively contributed to society. Conversely, domestic work is not viewed as a job when performed by a wife or female partner but often as a labor of love. Based upon this division of labor, femininity discourses position women as possessing a maternal instinct and thus predisposed to caregiving while men, who purportedly lack this instinct, are excused from full domestic involvement. Accordingly, femininity is associated with the private sphere of the home and masculinity with the public realm of the workplace. Stemming from these notions of masculinity and femininity, women end up performing the majority of domestic work and childcare regardless of their participation in the paid work force because they are positioned as caregivers.

The modern gender division of labor reflects the perniciousness of gender differences discourses and has significant implications for women's social position. Women may feel compelled to pursue motherhood full-time or enter *family-friendly* professions because of their husbands' non-involvement within the home. Similarly, employers may justify their decision to exclude women from positions of authority because purported family responsibilities are difficult to combine with the demands of the job. This rationale defines all women as mothers of young children, while most are not (Connell 1987, 80). Furthermore, this logic defines women and not men as parents, which legitimizes an unequal distribution of childcare and domestic responsibilities. Indeed, we see evidence of a *gendered accumulation process* (Connell 2009, 80) where men accrue material wealth and social prestige from their public role and women either remain entirely financially dependent upon a male breadwinner or pursue professions which incur inadequate financial compensation.

The modern gender division of labor is built upon an assumption of gender difference and hegemonic heterosexuality, both of which are related to emotional relations.

Emotional Relations

Gender differences discourses position men and women as not only predisposed to performing certain types of work but also as having different, albeit complementary, sexual desires, hence a logic of opposites attract. Contemporary Western societies distinguish between homosexual and heterosexual desire (Connell 2009, 82). Despite the existence of these two forms of sexual attachment, heterosexuality is socially sanctioned while homosexuality is denigrated. As a result, scholars refer to this as compulsory heterosexuality (Rich 1980) or hegemonic heterosexuality (Connell 1987, 113).

The term *heteronormativity* is also a pervasive component of emotional relations. Heteronormativity indexes heterosexuality's hegemonic grip on defining *normative* sexuality while alternative sexualities are pathologized (Baker 2008, 109; Cameron and Kulick 2006, 9). Heteronormativity extends beyond the normalization of heterosexuality to encompass the normalization of a certain type of heterosexuality that involves marriage and monogamy while single, nonmonogamous, or voluntarily celibate individuals are viewed as deviant (Cameron and Kulick 2006, 165). Heteronormativity is evident in a wide array of daily social practices such as an assumption that men and women marry and that women are monogamous and relationship-oriented while men are unfaithful and permissive.

Emotional relations also come into play in the arena of work. Many professions require their employees to form a particular emotional relationship with their employees (Connell 2009, 83). In reference to Hochschild's (1983) research, Connell cites the job of flight attendant where employees are trained to encourage customers to relax and debt collectors as requiring displays of verbal aggression. Clearly, the type of emotional relations the job requires of their employees is also gendered. We might associate flight attendants with femininity because they attend to the physical and emotional needs of their customers and debt collectors with masculinity because they display verbal bravado.

Power, production, and emotional relations are also embedded in the final dimension of gender relations, symbolic relations.

Symbolic Relations

The social construction of certain actions and behaviors as symbolically masculine or feminine is not neutral and value-free but infused with ideologies which position femininity as inferior to masculinity. We see evidence of this ideology in the symbolic construction of women as domestic caregivers and subsequent cultural denigration of domestic work. Full-time domestic work does not result in a paid wage, which is a symbol that an individual is making a meaningful social contribution.

The symbolic dimension of gender relations can be found in dress, makeup, and the media (Connell 2009, 84). For example, culturally idealized forms of femininity construct women as thin, young, and sexually appealing. Women attempt to embody this form of femininity through diet, cosmetics use, and adopting a certain style of dress. The cultural idealization of youth is evident in the media by the predominance of younger actresses and underrepresentation of older actresses. Notably, mature male actors are not only overrepresented in popular films, but also often paired with younger female actresses in nonplatonic relationships. Masculinity's superior position over femininity ensures that men become distinguished as they age while women simply age.

In distinguishing these four levels of gender relations, Connell is not suggesting that they operate in isolation from each other. Quite the contrary, there is a large degree of overlap and intersection. The relations between these four dimensions form the basis of gender regimes of particular social institutions and the overall gender order of a society.

A *gender regime* (Connell 1987, 120) refers to gender-based institutionalized power relations which allocate men and women to different social tasks and characterize specific social institutions (see also Bagilhole 2002, 165–66; Wajc-man, 1998, 3). We can speak of gender regimes of the family, schools, and corporations. Gender regimes are formed based upon the interaction between relations of power, production, emotional, and have symbolic dimensions. The gender regimes in a particular society constitute its overall *gender order* (Connell 1987, 134). The gender regimes of particular institutions usually dovetail the society's overall gender order, but this is not always the case. In-deed, *crisis tendencies*, which destabilize gender regimes, can serve as catalysts that induce change in a society's gender order. Crisis tendencies can be identi-fied in each of the four dimensions of gender relations (Connell 2009, 90).

Power relations have experienced crisis tendencies (Connell 1995, 85). Feminist movements and subsequent passage of equal employment opportuni-ties legislation have challenged and somewhat destabilized the legitimacy of a patriarchal gender order. However, women's lower income in relation to men's and underrepresentation in powerful positions within organizations indicates that the gender order has yet to experience a complete transformation.

Crisis tendencies have also disrupted production relations (Connell 1995, 85; 2009, 91). Women's increased participation in the paid labor force chal-lenges the ideology that men are family providers and women caregivers. Nevertheless, the expectation that professional women still manage the household can hinder their career prospects while men are ensured a smooth career trajectory, uninterrupted by domestic responsibilities.

Emotional relations have also been a site of crisis tendencies (Connell 1995, 85). Connell contends that although homosexuals are still targets of abuse and violence, homosexual sexuality has achieved a certain degree of cultural le-gitimacy in a gender order where heterosexuality is dominant. Connell cites visible gay and lesbian communities in many major metropolitan areas, anti-discrimination and anti-defamation laws, and we might add the legalization of homosexual marriages in some countries as examples to support the idea that emotional relations are experiencing crisis tendencies. In reference to heterosexual sexuality, women exhibit a greater degree of sexual freedom than before; however, a sexual double standard still operates which permits male sexual promiscuity but punishes women for comparable behavior.

The instability of patriarchy can be viewed as a crisis tendency within sym-bolic relations. Social movements such as women's liberation have challenged the conventional assumption that a woman's place is in the home. In contrast to the past, gender equality has become a cultural trope and those who claim otherwise have to defend their position. Despite these positive changes, I would argue that femininity discourses continue to disempower women. One only has to look at the media to find examples of singers and actresses whose talent remains secondary to their physical attractiveness and sexual appeal.

Conclusion

This chapter has demonstrated how gender is not a fixed trait, but is an active accomplishment which occurs within specific social and historical contexts and intersects with age, race, and social class. Although gender is fluid and socially constructed, men and women are held accountable to normative notions of masculinity and femininity. Individuals possess agency to practice gender in multiple ways; however, nonnormative gendered performances are usually noticed and negatively assessed (West and Zimmerman 1987, 136). For this reason, gender is best viewed as embodied structured action or gendered performances orchestrated to reflect social norms (Messerschmidt 2004, 40)

This chapter has also suggested that we need to look at macro-level processes which structure and thus curtail individuals' embodied gender performances. To incorporate the structural dimension into my conceptualization of gender, I discussed Connell's (1987, 2009) four-pronged gender relations approach. Connell maintains that the active accomplishment of gender intersects with and is thus shaped by the structural dynamics of power relations, production relations, emotional relations, and symbolic relations. Power relations reference the gender-based distribution of social resources such as material wealth and socially prestigious professions. Production relations are the type of labor which societies assign to men and women and the value assigned to that labor. Emotional relations index sexual orientation and the emotions that individuals are expected to display in certain professions. Symbolic relations are the meanings that we assign to the concepts masculinity and femininity. These four areas of gender relations are not separate entities but dynamically intersect with and thus influence each other.

Finally, the chapter discussed how gender relations are not stable and enduring but are rendered unstable and disrupted by crisis tendencies (Connell 2009, 90). Patriarchal gender relations, which benefit economically privileged white heterosexual men, have been destabilized and somewhat weakened by women's and gay liberation movements and the passage of equal employment and anti-discrimination legislation. Nonetheless, women are still collectively disadvantaged compared to men in terms of equal access to material wealth and control of institutionally powerful positions. Patriarchal gender relations have been weakened but not completely dissolved.

The next chapter will further investigate how social structures influence individuals' gender accomplishments. Specifically, I exemplify the complementary but unequal relationship definitive of hegemonic masculinity and hegemonic femininity and discuss the book's major theoretical concepts.

Crucially, I will demonstrate how a certain degree of power accompanies the embodiment hegemonic masculinity while a relative degree of powerlessness follows the embodiment of femininity. Hence, the symbolic construction of masculinity and femininity as fundamentally asymmetrical is a central mechanism through which a patriarchal gender order is legitimated and sustained.

2

Geographies of Femininities

As I have discussed, an essentialist assumption of dichotomous sex categories forms the basis of socially constructed notions regarding masculinity and femininity. However, gender is not only constructed from an assumption that men and women are naturally different but also from differences between members of the same sex. These differences lead to the formation of unequally valued masculinities and femininities. Some forms of masculinity and femininity are culturally idealized and celebrated while others are denigrated and stigmatized. In this chapter, I discuss both culturally exalted and marginalized masculinities and femininities but maintain a focus on femininities. More specifically, I discuss the concepts of emphasized, dominant, hegemonic, subordinate, and oppositional femininities, which form the basis of this book's analytical chapters.

Hegemonic Masculinities and Emphasized Femininities

Femininities and masculinities are situationally specific *embodied social actions* (Messerschmidt 2000, 2004), which constitute normative actions and behaviors that men and women are held accountable to. Masculine embodied social actions include demonstrating authority, control, independence, competitive individualism, aggressiveness, the capacity for violence, and permissive heterosexuality (Messerschmidt 2000, 10). Since difference is the cornerstone of masculinity and femininity, embodied social actions associated with femininity include compliance, dependence on others—particularly men—cooperative ability, passivity, and conservative sexuality. As social, situational, and historical variation exists, the listed embodied social actions are neither exhaustive nor fixed.

Despite the existence of multiple masculinities and femininities, they do not align on an equal playing field but exist in a hierarchical relationship of dominance and subordination (Connell 1987, 183–88; 1995, 77–81; Messerschmidt 2010, 35–40). The path-breaking concept of *hegemonic masculinity* refers to "the configuration of gender practice which embodies the currently accepted answer to the problem of the legitimacy of patriarchy, which guarantees (or is taken to guarantee) the dominant position of men and the subordination of women" (Connell 1995, 77). Crucially, the concept does not merely reference character traits but patterns of social practice that men mobilize in order to construct and sustain a hierarchical relationship between other men and women, masculinities and femininities. For instance, men may strive to occupy a superior position at work by emphasizing their abilities and exploiting others through taking credit for women's labor and undermining women (Martin 2001, 601). Crucially, masculine social practices are contextually available *masculine resources* (Messerschmidt 2000, 12) men mobilize to construe their masculinities and not simply a reflection of biology. Therefore, men are active agents in constructing multiple forms of masculinities.

Central to the concept of hegemonic masculinity is Gramsci's (1971) notion of hegemony, or the maintenance of power by the ruling class through obtaining consent rather than coercion (Connell and Messerschmidt 2005, 841, 846; Messerschmidt 2010, 26, 35). A state of gender hegemony exists when one form of masculinity achieves dominance over other subaltern masculinities and femininities. While simultaneously acknowledging that cultural, situational, and historical variation exists, hegemonic masculinity can be provisionally defined as a well-educated, white, middle-class, heterosexual breadwinner. As relationality is a central component of hegemonic masculinity, non–middle class, nonwhite, and nonheterosexual men are deemed subordinate to hegemonic masculinity. Most crucially for the purpose of this study, hegemonic masculinity is always constructed as superior to femininity. Notably, hegemonic masculinity's ascendance to power is contingent upon persuading the populace that asymmetrical gender relations are natural and inevitable. So many new fathers may automatically assume their wives take childcare leave and thus rearrange their professional lives while their careers remain unaffected. As a result, wives' domestic work supports men's upward mobility within the workplace and subsequent access to material wealth and institutional power. Thus, women play a crucial role in legitimating hegemonic masculinity and ensuring their own subordination.

There is often a discrepancy between hegemonic masculinities and men's actual embodied gendered actions (Connell and Messerschmidt 2005, 38–39, 46; Messerschmidt 2010, 22–23, 36). Notwithstanding, society-wide exemplars of hegemonic masculinities (e.g., professional athletes) can and do contribute to the process of maintaining an unequal gender order (gender hegemony). For instance, spectator sports are a popular leisure activity which unifies men of diverse ages and socioeconomic classes and notably excludes women (Kimmel 2006, 246; Messner 2007, 37). Arguably, discussions about sports are a contextually available *masculine resource* men can mobilize to form same-sex bonds, which subsequently exclude women and some men. The connection between sports and hegemonic masculinity is also evident in the business world where corporations sponsor sports events (Connell 2000, 52) and sports metaphors are used to describe exemplary employees (e.g., *team player*). Accordingly, some of the time-honored social practices associated with sports such as self-confidence and competitive aggressiveness are mobilized by men to subordinate others and achieve success.

Social embodiment is another essential element of a comprehensive formulation of hegemonic masculinity (Connell and Messerschmidt 2005, 851–52; Messerschmidt 2010, 42–44). Importantly, bodies are not simply passive recipients of sociological processes but are active agents in the construction of masculinity (Connell 2009, 66–71). Thus, men agentively utilize their bodies to play sports, take risks, and, most importantly, display their heterosexuality. In the process of performing these gendered actions, bodies are strengthened, injured, and inevitably weakened by the process of aging. The specific embodied social practices which constitute hegemonic masculinities are at once temporally and spatially specific, thus temporal and cultural variation is the norm, not the exception.

Hegemonic masculinity is neither static nor ossified but fluid and subject to reconstruction (Connell and Messerschmidt 2005, 852–53). For example, clerical work was originally performed by men but later the occupational category of secretary was classified as *women's work* (Connell 2009, 79). In the current information age, clerical work is once again being performed by men. Currently, computer literacy is a defining feature of middle and upper-class hegemonic masculinity. Note, however, that while hegemonic masculinity is no longer associated with heavy manual work, it is still associated with the ability to operate machinery and remnants of this connection exist with names such as PowerBook (Connell 1995, 55–56). Media representations have also changed from macho images such as Clint Eastwood, Sylvester Stallone, and Arnold Schwarzenegger to softer forms of masculinity embodied by Richard Gere, Brad Pitt, and Jude Law. Importantly, these icons only represent hegemonic masculinity if they establish and maintain unequal relationships between other men and women. The nature of hegemony can also change from male heroes who rescue helpless female victims to more assertive female characters who occupy a peripheral and thus subordinate role to men in the films. Thus, hegemonic masculinity's ability to transform and reconfigure over time is the means by which it continues to claim and sustain its ascendant position.

Despite the potential for cultural, situational, and historical variation in forms of hegemonic masculinity, heterosexuality and male superiority and feminine inferiority are cornerstone practices constituting hegemonic masculinity. Masculine superiority can materialize as the cultural subordination of effeminate and gay men, both of whom are targets of verbal and physical abuse. Epithets such as *fag* or *sissy* are resources boys use to stigmatize and dominate others, emphasize their heterosexuality, and ultimately distance themselves from femininity (Connell 1995, 78–79; Pascoe 2007, 52–83). The stigmatization and denigration of femininity and homosexuality stems from their association with weakness, and hegemonic masculinity is built upon the assumption of men's natural supremacy over women (and effeminate men) (Connell 1995, 83); thus, men must demonstrate their distance from both in order to embody and enact hegemonic masculinity. Although softer representations of hegemonic masculinity are circulating in the media and popular culture, these icons are unquestionably heterosexual and thus not merely different from but superior to femininity.

Connell and Messerschmidt (2005, 849–51) and Messerschmidt (2010, 41–42) have recently proposed a tripartite framework for investigating constructions of hegemonic masculinities. Hegemonic masculinities are *locally* constructed through face-to-face interaction within major social institutions such as families, schools, and workplace organizations. Hegemonic masculinities are also *regionally* construed at a society-wide level through film actors, politicians, and business executives. Regional hegemonic masculinities disseminate cultural frameworks of normative masculine social practices which individuals accept, contest, or reformulate and thereby construct masculinities at local levels. Finally, hegemonic masculinities are *globally* constructed in the arenas of international politics, business, and media.

Certainly these three levels do not operate in isolation but intersect and thus influence other levels. For instance, the regional level can infiltrate and thus influence gender practices at the local level. Indeed, movie stars and professional athletes serve as exemplary archetypes of hegemonic masculinity which boys and men use as models for their own embodied gendered actions. In the process of engaging in certain celebrated masculine social actions and legitimating their superiority over other masculine and feminine practices, boys and men can successfully embody and enact hegemonic masculinity. Arguably, the prevalence of virtual and transnational media also influence gender practices at regional and local levels. Although not to dispel or underemphasize the potential for regional and local variation, there are currently images of masculinity which circulate and are thus hegemonic at the global level.

Before shifting to a discussion of femininities, a distinction needs to be drawn between hegemonic masculinities and nonhegemonic dominant masculinities. *Dominant masculinities* refer to "the most powerful or the most widespread types in the sense of being the most celebrated, common, or current forms of masculinity in a particular social setting" (Messerschmidt 2010, 38). To the extent that dominant forms of masculinity do not legitimate and sustain a hierarchical relationship with other masculinities and femininities, they are nonhegemonic. For example, a popular high school jock who does not structure and legitimate hierarchical relationships with other boys and girls could constitute a dominant masculinity at the local level. Therefore, social practices such as expressing tolerance toward homosexuality, disparaging pornography, and expressing pride in one's girlfriend's accomplishments and ambitions collectively construct a nonhegemonic dominant masculinity. However, a jock embodies hegemonic masculinity if he participates in gay-baiting, makes misogynistic comments, and forms non-egalitarian romantic relationships. In this case, a particular form of masculinity is simultaneously dominant and hegemonic, but this is not always true. As these examples illustrate, it is a mistake to conflate dominant with hegemonic forms of masculinity because they are fundamentally different. Hegemonic masculinities always establish and sustain unequal relationships with nonhegemonic masculinities and femininities and thus involve subordination. In contrast, dominant masculinities are powerful in the sense of constituting exemplary forms of masculinity but nonhegemonic because they fail to legitimate gender inequality. I will later make a similar distinction between dominant and hegemonic femininities.

The concept of hegemonic masculinity has also faced criticisms (e.g., Demetriou 2001; Donaldson 1993; Lusher and Robins 2009), which Connell and Messerschmidt (2005) and Messerschmidt (2010) have thoroughly addressed. I am not going to rehearse the criticisms here but instead redirect and maintain a focus on femininities. Before discussing hegemonic and pariah femininities (Schippers 2007), I discuss their historical predecessor: emphasized femininity (Connell 1987).

In reflection of Connell's view of gender as hierarchical relations between masculinities and femininities, she developed the concept of *emphasized femininity* in tandem with hegemonic masculinity. Connell (1987) formulated the relationship between masculinities and femininities as "the global dominance of men over women" (183) and subsequently defined emphasized femininity as "compliance with this subordination and is oriented to accommodating the interests and desires of men" (183). In their reformulation of the concept of hegemonic masculinity, Connell and Messerschmidt (2005, 846–47) and Messerschmidt (2010, 36) reject this somewhat static view of gender relations on the basis that "it is now clearly inadequate to our understanding of relations among groups of men and forms of masculinity and of women's relations with dominant masculinities." Messerschmidt has further developed the concept of emphasized femininity and thus contributed to our understanding of women's role in sustaining unequal gender relations by subordinating other women.

Messerschmidt (2004) provides a broader and more expansive conceptualization of emphasized femininity than Connell's original formulation. According to Messerschmidt (forthcoming):

> Emphasized femininity therefore is a form of femininity that is practiced in a complimentary, compliant, and accommodating subordinate relationship with hegemonic masculinity. And it is the legitimation of this relationship of superordination and subordination whereby the meaning and essence of both hegemonic masculinity and emphasized femininity are revealed. (26–27)

As previously discussed, hegemonic masculinity and emphasized femininity are always conceptualized as a hierarchical relationship between superordinate and subordinate, thus the concepts are meaningless outside of this relationship (Messerschmidt forthcoming, 26–27). As a result, emphasized femininity must always be conceptualized vis-à-vis hegemonic masculinities and nonemphasized femininities.

Some of my earlier points about hegemonic masculinity are also applicable to emphasized femininity. First, emphasized femininity is historically and geographically mobile. For instance, upper-class women in Elizabethan England emphasized their femininity with pale skin while many white women today do so with a tan. Second, the embodiment of emphasized femininity is unfeasible for many women; however, it remains a salient cultural ideal which influences actually women's bodily practices. For example, many women are unable to live up to the stringent standards of femininity which emphasize youth and thinness and are set by the media and fashion industry; nevertheless, and importantly, some women may orient to the standards set by media representations. The booming diet, exercise, and cosmetics industries, which are based upon a principle that women's bodies are deficient and thus require repair, exemplify this point. As a result, social embodiment is crucial to any construction of emphasized femininities.

Connell (1987) is careful to point out that subjectivities outside emphasized femininity are available for women who refuse to assume a subordinate position vis-à-vis hegemonic masculinity. These other femininities "are defined centrally by strategies of resistance or forms of noncompliance. Others again are defined by complex strategic combinations of compliance, resistance and co-operation" (183–84). Ostensibly, lesbians, nuns, nerds, or masculine women provide examples of resistance or noncompliance since they minimize (versus emphasize) their femininity. Connell adds, "Marilyn Monroe was both archetype and satirist of emphasized femininity" (1987, 188), presumably because Monroe embodied both a compliant and resistant relationship with hegemonic masculinity. Monroe expressed self-confidence in her appearance and sexuality, but that sexual appeal was ultimately performed for a male gaze. Examples such as Marilyn Monroe are particularly insightful because they illustrate how individuals can embody characteristics which simultaneously constitute and resist emphasized femininity and thereby illustrate that femininities, like masculinities, are dynamic and can exhibit contradictions (Connell and Messerschmidt 2005, 852–53; Messerschmidt 2010, 44–46). I will return to the notion of alternative femininities with my discussion of *pariah* and *oppositional* femininities.

In addition to distinguishing emphasized femininities at the local, regional, and global levels, a distinction needs to be made between emphasized and dominant forms of femininity. *Dominant femininities* refer to "the most powerful and/or the most widespread type in the sense of being the most celebrated, common, or current form of femininity in a particular social setting" (Messerschmidt forthcoming, 27). For example, cheerleaders are physically attractive, athletic, and popular, thus representing a dominant form of femininity in many middle-class secondary school local contexts (Adams and Bettis 2003, 4–5; Merten 1996, 51). The 1990s saw the formation of all-star squads whose sole purpose was to compete, not support male athletes (Adams and Bettis 2003, 39). These cheerleaders still embody many locally and regionally celebrated elements of femininity, yet they do not support the ascendance of hegemonic masculinity, and therefore represent a dominant, not emphasized form of femininity. As discussed, a cornerstone feature of emphasized femininities is that they occupy an accommodating and thus subordinate position in relation to hegemonic masculinity and therein sustain asymmetrical gender relations. Dominant femininities are never emphasized unless they meet the criteria of occupying a subordinate position in relation to hegemonic masculinity. At the same time, dominant femininities must be conceptualized in relation to emphasized, subordinate, and oppositional femininities because they acquire meaning through relationships with other women (Messerschmidt forthcoming, 27).

Subordinate femininities are "those femininities situationally constructed as aberrant and deviant in relation to both emphasized and dominant femininities" (Messerschmidt forthcoming, 27). Subordination can occur along the lines of race, class, age, sexuality, bodily display, or behavior, and the individual is deemed unfeminine (Messerschmidt forthcoming, 27). Peer abuse is one example of the subordination that adolescent girls face for failing to embody a contextually bound form of dominant or emphasized femininity (see Messerschmidt 2004, forthcoming).

Bullying exemplifies a contextually available *feminine resource* (Messerschmidt 2004), which enables girls to simultaneously subordinate gender nonconforming girls and normalize certain gendered practices. Gender deviant girls are often the targets of and thus victimized by verbal and physical abuse and social isolation (Brown 2003; Merten 1997; Messerschmidt 2004, forthcoming). Indeed, some girls are unable to embody signifiers of dominant femininity such as slenderness, athleticism, and heterosexual desirability, and consequently embody a subordinate femininity in the gender regime of a school. Adolescents are not only victimized through verbal and physical peer abuse, but by "an oppressive hierarchically embodied relationship among girls that is institutionalized in schools" (Messerschmidt 2004, 84).

It is necessary to reemphasize that while emphasized femininities are superior to subordinate femininities, hegemonic masculinities always dominate emphasized femininities. As Connell originally stated, "all forms of femininity in this society are constructed in the context of the overall subordination of women to men. For this reason there is no femininity that holds among women the position held by hegemonic masculinity among men" (Connell 1987, 187). This claim still applies to many societies where men tend to earn larger salaries than women, monopolize social positions with institutional authority such as in politics and the corporate sector (Connell 2009, 132), and masculine characteristics are often the sine qua non of success in the public realm. Significantly, we see how women's power pales in comparison with men's and thus unequal gender relations remain normative.

A plethora of masculinities research has informed our understanding of the various ways men collectively benefit from maintaining a superior position vis-à-vis nonhegemonic masculinities and femininities (see Connell and Messerschmidt 2005; Messerschmidt 2010). Unfortunately, the relationship between hegemonic masculinity, emphasized femininity, and alternative femininities is still in the initial stages of being theoretically formulated and empirically investigated; therefore, women's role in reifying or resisting gender hegemony remains unclear. In their recent reformulation of hegemonic masculinity, Connell and Messerschmidt (2005, 848) and Messerschmidt (2010, 39) acknowledge this unfortunate situation:

> The concept of "emphasized femininity" focused on compliance to patriarchy, and this is still highly relevant in contemporary mass culture. Yet gender hierarchies are also impacted by new configurations of women's identity and practice,

especially among younger women—which are increasingly acknowledged by younger men. We consider that research on hegemonic masculinity now needs to give much closer attention to the practices of women and to the historical interplay of femininities and masculinities.

Schippers's (2007) model of hegemonic and pariah femininities represents one attempt to rectify this situation. Schippers proposes a model of gender relations which encompasses power relations between femininities, but does not ignore the overall subordinate status of femininity in relation to masculinity at the societal level. Schippers's model also incorporates the dynamic interrelationship between race, class, and gender, and offers much promise for the future of femininities research. I now turn to Schippers's (2007) formulation of hegemonic and pariah femininities in the next section.

Hegemonic, Pariah, and Oppositional Femininities

Schippers prefers the term *hegemonic* to *emphasized* femininity and conceptualizes heterosexual desire as the basis of culturally constructed notions of masculinity and femininity. Notably, in applying this term she is not suggesting that hegemonic masculinity and hegemonic femininity are equal; on the contrary, hegemonic masculinity is always superior to hegemonic femininity. Specifically, Schippers draws on Butler's (1999, 194) concept of the *heterosexual matrix*, which assumes heterosexuality as the structuring agent for gender and the asymmetrical relationship between masculinity and femininity (Schippers 2007, 89). In the heterosexual matrix, gender and heteronormativity work to construct men and women as two distinct classes of people. Certain activities, behaviors, and patterns of consumption tend to correspond to each category and consequently define masculinity and femininity (Schippers 2007, 90). The relationship between masculinity and femininity, then, is one of difference and complementarity because the differences between masculinity and femininity are complemented by heterosexual desire which fuses men and women together—masculinity is always associated with erotic desire for the feminine object and femininity with being the object of masculine desire (Schippers 2007, 90). Hegemony is maintained through constructing complementary but asymmetrical relational differences between men and women. For example, men are physically strong and authoritative while women are physically weak and submissive. Of greater importance, however, is Schippers's point that the relationship between masculinity and femininity extends beyond difference and instead revolves around an axis of dominance and submission.

Difference and complementarity alone, however, do not constitute a state of hegemony (Schippers 2007, 90). A state of hegemony exists when particular practices or behaviors which serve the interests of those in power are used to make the resulting unequal social order appear natural or inevitable. According to Schippers, one such practice is the construction of a dominant male and submissive female sexuality. Thus, men are seen as possessing a natural desire to dominate women through sexual intercourse. Wendy Hollway (1984, 231) refers to this phenomenon as a *male sexual drive* discourse which assumes that men's insatiable sexuality is a direct product of biology. Hence, a double standard exists where concupiscent men are complimented as *studs* or *lady's men*, while women who engage in the same behavior are stigmatized and denigrated as *sluts* and *whores*. In line with my earlier discussion, gender differences can be manipulated and obscured to maintain existing unequal social relations. Unfortunately, male perpetrators of sexual violence may be excused for doing what's natural while female victims are blamed for leading men on (Miller 2001, 191). Similarly, Connell (1987, 113) makes the insightful point that a double standard which sanctions male sexual promiscuity and forbids it to women is not rooted in biology but with men's greater power.

Schippers (2007, 93) conceptualizes the relationship between masculinity and femininity as symbolic; however and importantly, symbolic meanings can infiltrate and therefore influence material practices such as unequal divisions of domestic labor, power, wealth, and the cultural marginalization of homosexuality. Hegemonic masculinities and femininities can be built upon essentialist gender differences discourses which naturalize and sustain an unequal gender order. As previously discussed, gender differences discourses construct femininity as unsuitable for powerful positions within social institutions and therefore legitimize women's subordination. It is not coincidental or arbitrary that hegemonic femininity is associated with unpaid domestic labor and caregiving while hegemonic masculinity is associated with paid labor and socially prestigious positions. The complementary and hierarchical relationship between masculinity and femininity implies domination through consent and not force (i.e., hegemony).

As the above discussion has suggested, the relationship between masculinity and femininity is not only one of difference but also the asymmetricality of domination and submission. Schippers builds on Connell's (1987, 183) notion that hegemonic masculinity is constructed through the domination of femininity. *Hegemonic masculinity* is "the qualities defined as manly that establish and legitimate a hierarchical and complementary relationship to femininity and that, by doing so, guarantee the dominant position of men and subordination of women" (Schippers 2007, 94). In contrast, *hegemonic femininity* is "the characteristics defined as womanly that establish and legitimate a hierarchical and complementary relationship to hegemonic masculinity and that, by doing so, guarantee the dominant position of men and the subordination of women" (Schippers 2007, 94). These characteristics, of course, exhibit situational and cultural variation, intersect with age, social class, race, sexuality, and change over time. A significant difference between masculinity and femininity, however, is that while men are empowered through the embodiment of hegemonic masculinity, the celebrated characteristics associated with hegemonic femininity work to subordinate and ultimately disempower women, so for them it is a paradoxical privilege.

Schippers's definition of hegemonic femininity departs from Connell's claim that "femininity organized as an adaptation to men's power, and emphasizing compliance, nurturance, and empathy as womanly virtues, is not in much of a state to establish hegemony over other forms of femininity" (Connell 1987, 188). Importantly, Schippers offers a view of hegemonic masculinity as dominate over hegemonic femininity, yet also incorporates the potential for femininities to organize into hierarchal relationships. For example, in Messerschmidt's (2004) study of violent adolescents, *preppy femininity*, which emphasizes academic achievement and a conservative style of dress and sexuality, was ascendant or hegemonic within the social context of the school, while *badass femininity*, which prioritized truancy, drug and alcohol abuse, and a permissive style of dress and sexuality, was hegemonic within the social milieu of the street. Importantly, both forms of femininity formed an unequal relationship with hegemonic masculinity and therefore represented hegemonic femininities. Struggles for dominance between these two forms of femininity did occur within the school when preppy girls verbally abused a badass who responded with physical violence (Messerschmidt 2004, 89–92). This example illustrates that within the same social milieu two different forms of femininity can compete for dominance. Therefore, Schippers offers a more dynamic and nonessentialist view of power relations between femininities than Connell.

Following Messerschmidt (2010, 165), I take issue with Schippers's argument that masculinities are never subordinate. *Subordinated masculinities* (Connell 1995, 78–79) are gay or effeminate heterosexual men who are rendered gender deviant and consequently stigmatized because of a fundamental incongruence between their sex category and embodied gendered behavior. Schippers rejects this term and applies *male femininities* to encompass embodied male femininity because "there are no masculine characteristics that are stigmatized as contaminating or as subordinate" (Schippers 2007, 96), so men who embody elements of femininity are by definition nonmasculine. Schippers's dismissal of the concept of subordinated masculinities is problematic for two interrelated reasons. First, nonheterosexual sexuality is clearly subordinate in a heteronormative gender order, which venerates heterosexuality and marginalizes homosexuality. As Schippers (2007, 96) correctly points out, male erotic desire is associated with femininity; however, there are gay men who conform to most mandates of orthodox masculinity outside of sexuality. Certainly, these men embody a subordinate form of masculinity, not *male femininity*. For this reason, subordinate masculinity is a term which more adequately encapsulates the oppression of a whole range of gender deviant men. Second, male femininities fail to account for the existence of *toxic masculinities* (e.g., an evil masculine villain), who are in no way feminine but nonetheless subordinate to hegemonic masculinity (Messerschmidt 2010, 165). Messerschmidt's (2010) important study of the discourse of former presidents George H. W. Bush and George W. Bush provides invaluable insight into the process where heroic hegemonic masculinities are discursively constructed in relation to both villainous subordinate masculinities and victimized emphasized femininities. As previously stressed, the subordination of nonhegemonic masculinities and femininities is the main channel through which gender hegemony is constructed and maintained.

A conceptualization of hegemonic femininity remains incomplete without considering nonhegemonic forms of femininity. In Schippers's (2007, 95) model, hegemonic femininity is ascendant in relation to nonhegemonic or *pariah femininities*. Schippers contends that in order to maintain its dominant position, characteristics associated with hegemonic masculinity must remain the exclusive possession of men. Pariah femininities are women who embody aspects of hegemonic masculinity and by doing so refuse to occupy a subordinate position in relation to hegemonic masculinity. Significantly, pariah femininities threaten to dismantle the heterosexual matrix and remove hegemonic masculinity from its extolled position. Women who are assertive, sexually promiscuous, or nonheterosexual exemplify pariah femininities and can incur discursive sanctioning exemplified by derogatory epithets such as *bitch, slut,* and *dyke*. Schippers refers to these women as *pariah* in lieu of *subordinate* femininities to emphasize that they are not so much inferior to hegemonic femininity, but threaten to contaminate the asymmetrical relationship between masculinity and femininity and challenge the ascendant position of hegemonic masculinity.

Pariah femininities are women whose sex category membership misaligns with their embodied social actions. Importantly, these women are not trying to claim male sex category membership like the transsexual Agnes; nonetheless, they are denigrated and sanctioned for their gender deviance. Clearly, the slew of derogatory terms men use to sanction these women signals the threat they pose to hegemonic masculinity. These abusive terms resemble men's use of force in order to claim or sustain patriarchal privilege. In reference to men's use of violence, Connell (1995, 84) states, "violence is part of a system of domination, but it is also a measure of its imperfection. A thoroughly legitimate hierarchy would have less need to intimidate." Similarly, the slew of derogatory epithets used to stigmatize and sanction pariah femininities indicate the potential threat these women pose to hegemonic masculinity.

In line with my comments about masculinity, there are multiple configurations of hegemonic and pariah femininities which exhibit situational and cultural variation and intersect with age, race, social class, and sexuality; therefore, hegemonic femininity in one context could be pariah in another context. For instance, a stay-at-home mother could be a middle-class ideal of hegemonic femininity while a working woman who also balances the second shift of childcare and domestic responsibilities could be hegemonic in a working class context. Although participation in the workforce was originally a masculine embodied social action, working women perform the lion's share of domestic work (Hochschild 1989; Stone 2008; Wajcman 1998); thus hegemonic masculinity remains unchallenged.

The concept of pariah femininities captures the strong stigmatization of women who fail to embody hegemonic femininity. However, the concept carries strong negative connotations and for this reason I am adopting the term *oppositional femininities*. *Oppositional masculinities* are alternative, nonhegemonic masculinities that "in one way or another are extrinsic to and represent significant breaks from hegemonic masculinity, and may actually threaten its dominance" (Messerschmidt 2000, 12). Messerschmidt (forthcoming) later applies this definition to femininity and coins the term *oppositional femininities*, which captures the notion of resistance or noncompliance with hegemonic femininity but does not carry the negative semantic connotations of social outcast. I think that a broad conceptualization of all nonhegemonic femininities as pariah is overstated and fails to capture various manifestations of noncompliance. In contrast, oppositional femininities encompasses a wide range of femininities such as the sexually permissive or nonheterosexual women identified by Schippers, but can also apply to women who do not necessarily embody aspects of hegemonic masculinity but nonetheless resist or oppose elements of hegemonic femininity and thus the unequal relationship between hegemonic masculinity and hegemonic femininity. Nuns, celibate women, and single women exemplify this phenomenon. Unlike Schippers's pariah femininities, which refer to women who embody and enact aspects of hegemonic masculinity, oppositional femininities encompass women who challenge patriarchal gender relations through outright noncompliance and more subtle forms of resistance. In this book I will demonstrate how oppositional femininities resist hegemonic femininity in multifarious ways.

Due to the broad range of femininities encompassed by the term oppositional femininities, the specific aspects of hegemonic masculinity or hege-

monic femininity which oppositional femininities embody, subvert, or reformulate require further clarification. Schippers lists aggression, sexual
promiscuity, and homosexuality as defining elements of pariah femininities;
however, these are very different characteristics which should arguably remain separate for the purpose of clarifying resistance from accommodation.
For instance, physically violent women subvert hegemonic femininity by embodying a toxic element associated with hegemonic masculinity, but problematically do not challenge the legitimacy of the utilization of physical force
as a means to claim power over others. Other oppositional femininities, by
contrast, subvert aspects of hegemonic femininity but do not reaffirm the legitimacy of toxic hegemonic masculine values and thus may contribute to
equalizing gender relations and provide women with a politics of resistance. I
next distinguish between these two forms of oppositional femininities.

Lesbians unsettle the basis of both hegemonic masculinity and heteronormativity by rejecting compulsory heterosexuality. Unlike heterosexual women,
who are the object of men's sexual desire, lesbian sexuality positions women as
both subjects and objects of sexual desire and thus empowers women. Women
are not relegated to the passive position of sexual object but repositioned as
agents of their own sexuality. Thus lesbians can both be pursued but also pursue the objects of their sexual desire. Of equal importance, lesbians challenge
an assumption of heteronormativity which underpins normative sexuality in
contemporary American society. That is, they challenge the heterosexual matrix which positions men and women as different but complementary categories. Notably, however, lesbian sexuality is not a position with power equivalent to male heterosexuality due to the overall social marginalization and
denigration of homosexuality. Therefore, the disruptive potential of lesbian
sexuality stems not from its association with hegemonic masculinity, but from
the possibility of transforming a heteronormative gender order.

Single women have the potential to disrupt both hegemonic heterosexuality and production relations. Similar to lesbians, their power comes from the
challenge they pose to hegemonic masculinity by rejecting the social institution of marriage. Single women can be seen as contributing to changing a
patriarchal gender order as they challenge the basis of heteronormativity and
assumption that men financially support women.

Both heterosexually and homosexually promiscuous women challenge an
assumption of passive female sexuality. In addition to identifying a male sexual
drive discourse, Hollway (1984) also identified a *permissive* discourse which is
theoretically available to members of both sexes. Nevertheless, hegemonic
definitions of monogamous female sexuality make this discourse difficult for
women to engage with. The power of permissive sexuality arises from its association with hegemonic masculinity; however, this is not necessarily a trans-

gressive gender practice. Narratives about alleged sexual conquests become a resource men use to simultaneously compete with other men and embody hegemonic masculinity (Kimmel 2008, 206–7). Most likely sexual-conquest narratives will not become a resource women use to embody femininity; however, the practice itself reifies versus subverts a patriarchal gender order.

Physically violent or aggressive women challenge a presumption that women are physically and emotionally vulnerable. This gendered stereotype penetrates aspects of social life such as the workplace where women are rendered unsuitable for certain masculine professions. As my chapter on the workplace will illustrate, aggression is a defining feature of professional success in many masculinized professions such as business and law enforcement. In contradistinction, feminine characteristics such as collaboration and empathy are conveniently removed from a definition of professional success in order to simultaneously exclude women from these socially prestigious professions and ensure that masculinity occupies a superior position in relation to femininity. The power of both aggression and violence stems from their association with hegemonic masculinity; however, they are not positive characteristics and therefore cannot be seen as contributing to transforming a patriarchal gender order. The power garnered from aggression and violence involves constructing relationships of dominance and subordination which sustains versus subverts a patriarchal gender order.

Oppositional femininities can be seen as contributing to the formation of crisis tendencies in the current gender order. Professionally successful women unsettle the strong association between masculinity and paid labor and thereby contribute to the formation of crisis tendencies in power and production relations. Lesbians and single women challenge the basis of heteronormativity and therefore challenge emotional relations. Sexually assertive women challenge a passive female sexuality norm which also contests emotional relations. More broadly, oppositional femininities also contribute to the formation of crisis tendencies in symbolic relations by subverting hegemonic femininity through embodying elements of hegemonic masculinity or contesting hegemonic feminine social practices.

The above discussion has indicated that we can broadly distinguish between two types of oppositional femininities. First, there are oppositional femininities which form nonhierarchical and sometimes noncomplementary relationships with hegemonic masculinities and in the process contribute to democratizing gender relations. We can refer to these women as *equality femininities,* "those that are harmless and/or legitimate an egalitarian relationship between men and women, masculinity and femininity" (Messerschmidt 2010, 161). Equality femininities democratize gender relations not through practicing masculinity but by resisting disempowering feminine practices constituting hegemonic femininity and in the process equalize gender relations. Lesbians exemplify equality femininities as they disrupt heteronormativity, which positions men and women, masculinity and femininity, as complementary, but unequal opposites that are fused together by heterosexual desire. Hence, an active male sexuality is complemented by a passive female sexuality. Sexist gendered ideologies not only position men as aggressors in heterosexual relationships but also sanction sexual promiscuity in men and stigmatize it in women. By contesting sexist gendered ideologies about female sexuality and the heterosexual matrix, lesbians contribute to equalizing gender relations.

The second form of oppositional femininity subverts hegemonic femininity by engaging in toxic masculine practices such as peer bullying and arguably plays a role in sustaining and legitimizing these gender practices. Although these women clearly access a degree of power by drawing on a masculine practice, their gendered behavior supports the naturalization of a toxic masculine practice and sustains the formation of hierarchical relationships.

Finally, it is necessary to mention that dominant and subordinate femininities can also be oppositional. Dominant femininities embody the most common, celebrated, or widespread elements of hegemonic femininity, yet do not instantiate a hierarchical relationship between women and men, femininity and masculinity. We can conceptualize girls on competition-only cheerleading squads as representing dominant oppositional femininities within the local context of secondary schools. These girls embody many of the conventional markers of dominant femininity such as heterosexual appeal and athleticism; however, they do accommodate and thus form a subordinate relationship with hegemonic masculinity. Rather, these cheerleaders contest the unequal relationship between male athletes, who occupy the central and most important position in the game, and female cheerleaders, who are relegated to the sidelines. As the traditional athlete-cheerleader relationship parallels that of hegemonic masculinity and hegemonic femininity, competitive cheerleading squads challenge and potentially dismantle this hierarchical relationship. To the extent that dominant oppositional femininities subordinate and thus maintain unequal relations with other girls, we cannot conceptualize them as equality femininities.

Likewise, subordinate femininities can concomitantly be oppositional if they refuse to complement hegemonic masculinity. For instance, adolescent nerds are subordinate in relation to both dominant and hegemonic femininities in secondary schools for failing to embody most of the conventional markers of white, middle-class heterofemininity, such as heterosexual desirability, athleticism, and bodily adornment (see Adams et al. 2005; Bettis and Adams 2009). Simultaneously, they are oppositional since their academic overachievement, participation in unprestigious extracurricular activities (e.g., chess club), and apathy toward forming nonplatonic heterosexual relationships allows them to form equal relationships with boys. Indeed, their apparent indifference toward and thus disaffiliation with conventional markers of femininity and heterosexual desirability enables them to compete equally with their male peers in academic subjects such as mathematics and science where male dominance is normative (Bucholtz 1998, 124). Bucholtz (1998, 120; 2001, 85) rightly argues against the common view that nerds are simply social rejects and instead proposes that they are conscious resistors of mainstream adolescent cultural practices. Accordingly, we can view nerds as oppositional in relation to hegemonic femininity and its unequal relationship with hegemonic masculinity but simultaneously subordinate in relation to dominant and hegemonic femininities.

The theoretical frameworks outlined by Connell, Messerschmidt, and Schippers provide a useful tool to investigate the construction of femininities and thus provide valuable insight into femininity's role in supporting the ascendance of hegemonic masculinity. Hegemonic femininities serve as handmaidens which support the ascendance of hegemonic masculinity through occupying a complementary but subordinate position. In contradistinction, gender nonconforming oppositional femininities challenge the asymmetrical relationship definitive of hegemonic masculinity and hegemonic femininity. The existence of dominant, hegemonic, oppositional, and subordinate femininities indicate that individuals possess agency to construct different feminine identities. Oppositional femininities illustrate Connell's (1995, 37) point that no hegemony is totalitarian but can be contested and potentially disrupted or transformed. Due to their transformative potential, oppositional femininities may provide women empowerment and a politics of resistance.

Dominant Femininities

The concepts of dominant, hegemonic, subordinate, and oppositional femininities provide us with theoretical constructs to empirically examine the construction of various femininities within the social institutions of school, work, and the media. First, however, it is necessary to provisionally identify certain gendered practices which constitute dominant femininities. A dominant form of femininity can simultaneously be hegemonic if it legitimizes a hierarchical and complementary relationship with hegemonic masculinity. Again, it cannot be overstated that the characteristics I am identifying are nonexclusive, situationally and culturally variant, and historically mobile. In what follows, I outline some of the major characteristics which constitute white, middle-class dominant femininity.

Physical Appearance

Thinness can be seen as a defining element of contemporary dominant femininity. The pervasiveness of this ideal is reflected in print, visual, and virtual media which project images of emaciated women that serve as cultural ideals for individual women to measure themselves against and attempt to emulate. This cultural ideal can be seen across the board from seemingly harmless animation to films which target more mature audiences. Women's magazines are particularly noteworthy because they construct the female body as constantly requiring self-surveillance and repair through diet and the use of cosmetics and anti-aging creams (Gill 2007, 187; Wolf 1991, 65). Eating disorders are a devastating consequence of the cultural idealization of thinness. Importantly, women who suffer from anorexia nervosa are not mentally ill but rather gender conformists who attempt to embody a dominant femininity. Naomi Wolf (1991) raises the insightful point that the cultural ideal of thinness does not reflect a preoccupation with beauty but with female obedience (187). Therefore, the emaciated body of an anorexic woman is a symbol of self-control, discipline, and ultimately conformity to the rigid standards of dominant femininity.

Youth is another cornerstone feature constituting dominant femininity in many contexts. This ideal is particularly salient in the music and film industries. A double standard exists where gray hair and wrinkles distinguish men but marginalize women who then attempt to conceal visible signs of aging (Dull and West 2002, 135). Indeed, mature male actors are frequently paired with younger women but the reverse case is extremely rare. The booming cosmetic surgery industry can be seen as an extreme manifestation of a culture which equates youth with beauty.

A view of the female body as a project which requires continual improvement and renewal is reflected in a seminal study conducted by Dull and West (2002). The authors carried out interviews with cosmetic surgery surgeons and former patients and maintain that the interviewees' accounts about cosmetic surgery are inextricably linked to the accomplishment of gender. For example, surgeons claimed that women's desire to undergo surgery was unremarkable because cultural norms dictate that women should care about their appearance. Patients seemingly internalized this norm because they trivialized the significance of cosmetic surgery by comparing it to wearing makeup (Dull and West 2002, 134). Dull and West argue that a cultural conception of women's bodies as requiring repair draws on a natural differences argument which effectively constructs the decision to have surgery as a moral imperative versus aesthetic option (136). Therefore, cosmetic surgery is undertaken not simply for the purpose of aesthetic improvement, which could reflect personal vanity, but to repair a *defective* body.

Dull and West's study illustrates how cultural norms about femininity encourage women to self-monitor their appearance and even engage in expensive and potentially dangerous cosmetic procedures. Similar to how excessive dieting or exercising can damage an individual's health, cosmetic procedures can go awry and permanently damage one's health or appearance. Lamb and Brown (2006, 14) raise the important point that social norms teach girls that appearance is more important than what they can do. Lamb and Brown's comment is in reference to *fashionable* clothes such as tight jeans and shirts which restrict movement and thus discourage activity. Similarly, cultural norms which maintain that women's bodies are imperfect and require improvement suggest that a woman's appearance is more important than her capabilities.

Women can attempt to embody a dominant femininity through diet and exercise and attempt to preserve a youthful appearance; however, heterosexual appeal can be seen as a cornerstone element of dominant femininity. Therefore, femininity is constructed not only through individual body-management practices but also through men's appraisal of women. Despite women's efforts to modify their bodies, men possess the power to evaluate their physical attractiveness and therefore are powerfully positioned as the judges of women's sexual appeal.

Sexuality

Reflecting essentialist notions of gender differences, female sexuality is socially constructed as passive and male sexuality as active (Weedon 1987, 35). This bifurcation of male and female sexuality rests on a presumption of heterosexuality. Women are viewed as seeking committed heterosexual relationships while men are seen as sexual predators (Tolman 2002, 5). As I previously discussed, a male sexual drive discourse normalizes pernicious male sexuality while a permissive discourse, which is theoretically available to both men and women, is difficult for women to engage with. Therefore, women are confronted with a sexual double standard where they are expected to be sexually appealing but not overly sexual, lest they risk being labeled a *slut* or *whore* (Eder 1995, 129). The absence of discourses which construct female sexuality as active and desiring indicates that the virgin/whore dichotomy continues to prevail in contemporary American society (Brown 2003, 103; Tolman 2002, 11) and can repress women's sexual agency.

Self-Confidence

Reflecting a gendered ideology of complementary differences, which underpins the relationship between hegemonic masculinity and hegemonic femi-

ninity, cultural norms discourage and stigmatize women who are overconfident and overambitious. Whereas men are rewarded for exhibiting
self-confidence through terms such as *assertive, go-getter,* and *stud,* women are
viewed as overstepping the boundaries of conventional femininity and accordingly face disparaging epithets such as *aggressive, bitch,* or *slut* (Schippers
2007, 95). Confidence and ambition are arguably essential characteristics for
those aspiring to succeed. Significantly, the disparagement of confidence and
ambition in women illustrates how success confirms masculinity but disconfirms femininity (Kimmel 2008, 251). This double standard will become
clearer when I discuss the dilemma facing women who are stigmatized for
exhibiting strong leadership ability and professional competence.

A slender, youthful, and sexually desirable body and not overassertive personality can be seen as cornerstone elements of dominant femininity within
white, middle-class American society. These gendered practices simultaneously constitute hegemonic femininity if they are mobilized to construct and
maintain an unequal relationship between men and women, masculinity and
femininity. Certainly women are not coerced to inculcate images of hegemonic femininity promoted by the media and popular culture, but actively
choose to adorn and sculpt their bodies in various ways, which reifies the ascendancy of these images and sometimes contributes to their subordination.
Indeed, women can even be seen as possessing a certain degree of power exhibited by their capacity to purchase diet and fashion-related products. Nonetheless, there is a fundamental difference between the accomplishment of
hegemonic masculinity and hegemonic femininity. Whereas hegemonic masculinity is accomplished through personal effort and ability, hegemonic femininity is performed for and ultimately contingent upon men's validation. The
ultimate symbol that a woman has successfully embodied hegemonic femininity is securing a nonplatonic heterosexual relationship. I expand upon this
point in the next chapter with my discussion of the importance of heterosexual relationships in secondary schools.

Conclusion

In this chapter I further set out the book's theoretical framework by discussing the influential concepts of dominant, hegemonic, subordinate, and oppositional femininities. We saw how the heterosexual matrix is the structuring
agent for the relationship between hegemonic masculinity and hegemonic
femininity. Different but complementary social actions and behaviors cou-
pled with heteronormativity supposedly form the basis of the complementary
relationship between men and women, masculinity and femininity. Notably,

however, the relationship between hegemonic masculinity and femininity is not built upon principles of mutual compatibility and equality, but rather on the dominance of masculinity and subordination of femininity.

Crucially, a salient difference between hegemonic masculinity and hegemonic femininity is that men are empowered through embodying hegemonic masculinity, while women are disempowered by embodying hegemonic femininity. Concomitantly, the gender practices which constitute hegemonic femininity legitimate a hierarchical relationship with hegemonic masculinity and contribute to women's subordination. Practicing hegemonic femininity provides women with a socially legitimated gender identity, but they are disempowered in the process, which illustrates how practicing hegemonic femininity is women's paradoxical privilege.

Oppositional femininities refer to women who contest the unequal relationship between hegemonic masculinity and hegemonic femininity. Although certain forms of oppositional femininities accrue a certain degree of power through engaging in gender practices associated with hegemonic masculinity, I suggested that a distinction needs to be made between oppositional femininities who reify versus subvert hegemonic masculinity and thereby contribute to potentially equalizing gender relations.

In the final section of the chapter, I provisionally identified some characteristics constituting white, middle-class dominant femininity. A dominant form of femininity can simultaneously be hegemonic if it is subordinate to a hegemonic form of masculinity. I provisionally identified thinness, youth, passive sexuality, and subdued self-confidence as gendered characteristics comprising white, middle-class femininity. Images of dominant and hegemonic forms of femininity are projected by the film, fashion, and beauty industries and serve as models for actual women who attempt to emulate these ideals through diet, exercise, and consumption. As the next chapter will illustrate, girls also contribute to the ascendance of certain images not only through idealizing media images but also by marginalizing other girls who step outside the constrictive boundaries of normative femininity.

3

The Social Construction
of Femininities in School

Socialization within the institution of school commences in childhood and extends through young adulthood. Just as parents both explicitly and implicitly communicate ideas about gender to their children, schools also play a pivotal role in the process of constructing and mobilizing gender ideologies and thus can be seen as strongly gendered social institutions. The purpose of this chapter is to trace the process where dominant, hegemonic, subordinate, and oppositional femininities are constructed within gender regimes found in schools. I specifically focus on the period of adolescence and young adulthood because during this time a girl's popularity is not contingent upon her individual accomplishments or achievements but on the status of her boyfriend (Eckert and McConnell-Ginet 1995, 486; Kimmel 2008, 245–46). Therefore, the ability to secure a heterosexual relationship with a high-status boy is integral to successfully accomplish hegemonic and sometimes dominant forms of femininity. More significantly, heterosexuality reflects a norm that men and women are inherently different and becomes the basis for men's and women's social roles within the social institutions of school, workplace, and the media. This chapter will demonstrate how femininities are constructed through expectations about individuals' behavior both inside and outside the classroom.

Social Culture of Schools

Eckert and McConnell-Ginet (1995, 472) make the insightful point that significant parallels can be drawn between the social organization of public high schools and corporate institutions. High schools in the United States can be seen as *total institutions* (Goffman 1961, 4), which provide both academic instruction and an array of social activities such as organized sports and clubs. Similar to how informal networks and camaraderie are crucial to secure promotion and ultimately success within the corporate world, achievement within school is contingent upon both academic success and participation in the social culture. Crucially, students' engagement in extracurricular activities divides by gender which mirrors the gender division of labor in society (Eckert 2005, 384). Similar to how nondomestic work is socially valued while domestic work is devalued, gendered activities receive unequal value on the social marketplace of schools. Boys participate in institutionally sanctioned athletics, which are officially recognized through pep rallies, homecoming games, and uniforms that demarcate team membership and arguably a high level of prestige. Girls, by contrast, are overwhelmingly cheerleaders, athletes, performers in school plays, and organizers of social events, such as school dances and bake sales, which sustain the overall social climate of the institution but receive disparate recognition.

Although sports prowess is typically deemed a masculine social practice (Adams et al. 2005, 17; Kimmel 2006, 246), athletic involvement is now an integral component of dominant femininities in the local context of many secondary schools (Bettis and Adams 2009, 9); thus an athlete's fit, toned body is indeed an icon of dominant femininity. Nevertheless, female athletes remain accountable to femininity, so they carefully balance engaging in sports with displaying an appropriate feminine demeanor (Krane 2001, 116). Athletes can resolve this dilemma by becoming *heterosexy athletes* who exude their femininity through long hair, makeup, and, most importantly, heterosexuality (Adams et al. 2005, 21). Off the playing field, they are members of Homecoming Court, cheerleaders, prom queens, and beauty pageant contestants (Adams et al. 2005, 25). In contrast to other sports, cheerleading is an extracurricular activity which is strongly associated with dominant femininity, so cheerleaders do not risk disparaging labels such as *lesbian* or *dyke*.

The cheerleader is often cited as a prevalent signifier of adolescent femininity, and the jock/cheerleader couple receives peer sanctioning and valorization within secondary schools (Adams and Bettis 2003, 4); however, this norm is gradually changing. As I previously discussed, the 1990s saw the formation of all-star cheerleading squads whose primary function is to compete, not support male athletics (Adams and Bettis 2003, 39). In spite of this positive development, cheerleading remains strongly heterosexualized, so cheerleaders do not have to negotiate a *heterosexy athlete* identity (Adams and Bettis 2003, 71). The sexualization of cheerleaders also surfaces in popular media such as the critically acclaimed *American Beauty*, where an adolescent cheerleader is the object of the middle-aged protagonist's sexual fantasy. Furthermore, some of the idealized qualities in cheerleaders include attractiveness, a nice figure, and social adeptness (Adams and Bettis 2003, 34). Problematically, characteristics such as physical strength and endurance are exempt from this list, which supports research findings that physical appearance and sociability versus ability and accomplishments are often valorized in women (Eckert and McConnell-Ginet 1995, 491). Due to the sexualization of cheerleaders and supportive function of most squads, the emancipatory potential of cheerleading is debatable.

The fact that athletics are no longer an exclusively male domain can be viewed as a positive development toward democratizing asymmetrical gender relations. Notwithstanding, there are significant ways girls are still subordinated within the gender regimes of secondary schools. For example, female athletics overwhelmingly receive a disproportional amount of social prestige and institutional support compared with male sports (Eckert and McConnell-Ginet 1995, 485; Krane 2008, 159), thereby reflecting the superior status of masculinity and inferior status of femininity. Regarding cheerleading, the main purpose of the majority of squads is not to compete but support male-dominated interscholastic athletics (Adams and Bettis 2003, 63); thus women are relegated to the sidelines while men assume center stage. Finally, many of cheerleaders' main duties such as decorating lockers, preparing treat bags, and making signs for athletes (Adams and Bettis 2003, 40) are similar to domestic work in the sense that they are unrecognized and arguably undervalued supportive tasks. Collectively, these examples illustrate how boys receive public recognition and increased status through participation in sports and holding key positions within school government while girls are relegated to the sidelines as cheerleaders or organizers of social events (Eckert and McConnell-Ginet 1995, 476).

Social relations within the school are built upon an assumption of presumed heterosexuality which is observable in informal dating and institutionally sanctioned heterosexual pairings such as prom king and prom queen. Eckert and McConnell-Ginet (1995, 476) maintain that the jock/cheerleader relationship is replicated in the corporate world by a business executive and stay-at-home wife, but also acknowledge that this is changing. The symbolic jock/cheerleader pairing and associated embodied social actions also mirrors a more recent gender division of labor where overextended supermoms attempt to simultaneously juggle the competing requirements of home and work while fathers are allowed to indisputably privilege their careers (Bagilhole 2002, 135; Pyke 1996, 533; Wacjman 1998, 26).

Compulsory heterosexuality infiltrates many aspects of school social life and influences students' relationships. A *heterosexual market* (Eckert and

McConnell-Ginet 2003, 26–27) emerges in high schools where individuals' market value and gender intersect. Unlike boys, whose market value increases through participation in athletics and student government, girls' value is measured by and contingent upon their attractiveness, personality, and social adeptness, which are feminine resources that can be used to secure heterosexual alliances (Eckert and McConnell-Ginet 1995, 491). A fundamental disparity emerges in high school where boys' popularity is tied to personal accomplishments such as athletic prowess and positions in student government, while girls' popularity is contingent upon their success in navigating the heterosexual market and can involve alienating other girls. Ideologies of femininity discourage explicit acts of aggression by girls, so they must devise covert tactics to sabotage other girls but maintain a façade of harmony.

One such tactic is what psychologists call *relational aggression*, an indirect form of aggression characterized by behaviors such as gossiping and spreading rumors (Brown 2003, 16). Similarly, Eckert (2005, 385) discusses how adolescent girls construct and enforce rigid social boundaries through the development of cliques, which ostracize certain girls, and contemptuously develop a social resilience that is comparable to boys' physical or athletic toughness. Relational aggression or *girlfighting* (Brown 2003) is a form of psychological warfare girls engage in that exemplifies the social toughness they develop as they negotiate their value on the heterosexual market. Specific manifestations of girlfighting include disparaging labels and vicious talk about other girls' appearances.

Slut is an example of a stigmatizing label that is frequently used during girlfighting. Notably, slut is unrelated to actual sexual behavior but is a technique to seek revenge against girls who are too popular or threatening in some way (Brown 2003, 116). Girls who reach puberty early are prime targets of this epithet because they become the objects of boys' attention and thus threaten later developing girls (Brown 2003, 117). Adolescent girls face a difficult dilemma where popular styles such as spaghetti-strap tops and skintight jeans accentuate female sexuality but cultural norms constituting dominant forms of femininity condemn explicit displays of sexuality. Therefore, *slut* reflects the previously discussed sexual double standard where permissive sexuality is a source of masculine capital for men, but sullies women's reputations and decreases their value on the heterosexual market. The unfortunate consequence of this moniker is that it not only overemphasizes female sexuality while glossing over other characteristics, but also sustains a sexual double standard.

As I discussed in chapter 2, thinness is a definitive feature of hegemonic femininity. Therefore, *fat* is a verbal indication that a girl has transgressed the boundaries of normative femininity. Brown (2003, 122) claims that the devastating consequences of the *fat* label are equivalent to boys who are stigmatized as feminine. Both *fat* and *fag* can be seen as the antithesis of dominant notions of femininity and masculinity. Disturbingly, fat talk exemplifies our culture's fixation on physical perfection in girls and women and implies that a girl's appearance supersedes individual abilities or personality.

Bitch is a term that boys and girls alike apply to girls who are controlling, mean, and aggressive (Brown 2003, 124). Clearly these are negative character-istics; however, they are arguably a source of masculine capital for boys but denigration for girls. More significantly, however, *bitch* also refers to girls who exhibit too much confidence and ambition, which are cornerstone features of hegemonic masculinity and therefore subversive when women display them.

Eckert (2005, 388) astutely points out how labels are a powerful regulatory force which produce and sustain social categories. Thus, *slut, bitch,* and *fat talk* simultaneously define dominant femininity and reaffirm its boundaries through punishing and subordinating individuals who transgress its borders. Notably, *slut* and *bitch* index women who embody aspects of hegemonic mas-culinity which must remain inaccessible to women (Schippers 2007, 96). Surprisingly, girls are seemingly unaware of the devastating consequences of rigidly defining and enforcing notions of femininity. Girlfighting destroys potential alliances with other girls which could be empowering and instead contributes to the overall cultural marginalization of femininity and women, thus women become the foot soldiers of their own subordination.

Brown (2003, 140) suggests that the media and popular culture send a mes-sage to girls that other girls are untrustworthy and therefore that they should prioritize romantic heterosexual relationships before same-sex friendships. This cultural script plays out in Disney films where Cinderella, Snow White, and Sleeping Beauty reject relationships with other women who are portrayed as deceitful and find security and intimacy through heterosexual romance (Brown 2003, 145). Disturbingly, these films and the subterranean world of girlfighting together send a powerful, misogynistic message that other girls are untrustworthy and that relationships with girlfriends are always secondary to those with boyfriends.

Since a girl's popularity within the gender regime of the school is contin-gent upon securing a long-term heterosexual relationship, girlfighting can be conceptualized as a feminine resource that allows girls to concomitantly com-pete among themselves without transgressing the boundaries of dominant femininity, which condemns explicit displays of anger or aggression. Similar to how boys embody dominant masculinity through the use of physical ag-gression and constructing hierarchies of power and privilege, girlfighting is a strategy girls use to negotiate a place in continually shifting same-sex hierar-chical relationships. Significantly, however, relational aggression is funda-mentally gendered and reflective of girls' subordinate position in the gender regime of high school. Cultural scripts of dominant femininity both prohibit girls' use of direct aggression and construct femininity as involving hetero-sexual romance and thus dependence on a man. In contrast, ideologies of dominant masculinity license the use of direct aggression, sexual promiscuity, and ultimately independence. The emergent heterosexual market and non-egalitarian gender regimes found in schools are fundamentally patriarchal and thus mirror other social institutions.

The practice of girlfighting illustrates how dominant forms of femininity are constructed not only through engaging in certain feminine practices but also through policing and subordinating gender aberrant girls and sometimes boys (Messerschmidt forthcoming, 28). Disparaging labels and fat talk not only contribute to setting rigid standards of dominant femininity but also inhibit the recognition and acceptance of diverse femininities and thus create unequal relations among girls (Messerschmidt forthcoming, 28). Likewise, girls who label nonmasculine boys *fags* in order to capture popular boys' attention participate in a misogynistic practice and contribute to the overall cultural denigration of femininity. Notably, the term *fag* is applied to effeminate boys whose sex category and embodied social actions misalign and unmistakably reflects the overall cultural repudiation of femininity (Kimmel 2008, 76–77; Pascoe 2007, 58–59). Both girlfighting and gay-baiting prevent the formation of healthy alliances with gender nonconforming girls and boys with whom *popular* girls could form partnerships and collectively challenge the superordinate position of hegemonic masculinity and subordinate position of nonhegemonic masculinities and femininities.

I think it also needs to be stated that girlfighting and the construction of dominant and subordinate forms of femininity simultaneously contribute to the superior position of masculinity and inferior position of femininity. By dispelling disparaging labels such as *bitch* and *slut* to subordinate other girls for exhibiting confidence and ambition, they are punishing their peers for engaging in potentially empowering gender practices. My discussion of the classroom context will indicate that criteria for academic success often include confident self-expression. Furthermore, the absence of a masculine label equivalent to *slut* also contributes to sustaining unequal gender relations by condoning male and denouncing female promiscuity. This discussion has illustrated that the girlfighting is a feminine resource girls utilize in order to practice both dominant and hegemonic forms of femininity.

Tina: Bad-girl Subordinate Oppositional Femininity

Although dominant femininity ideologies position certain embodied social actions as normative and others as deviant, girls can contest these norms and construct alternative femininities. Nevertheless, since individuals are accountable to masculinity and femininity, transgression occurs alongside the risk of gender assessment and marginalization by others (West and Zimmerman 1987, 136). Messerschmidt's (2004) study of adolescent violence demonstrates how individuals can eschew gendered social practices which constitute hegemonic femininity and in the process construct oppositional femininity gender projects.

Tina was a working-class girl who originally embodied preppy hegemonic femininity within the gender regime of school. Tina's style of dress, conservative sexual demeanor, and decent academic record exemplify her original acceptance of the school culture and thus embodiment of hegemonic femininity at school. At home, Tina assisted her mother with domestic work and accepted a conventional division of domestic labor, which provides further evidence that she originally embarked on an essentially hegemonic femininity gender project.

The domestic violence that Tina's mother endured can be seen as the catalyst which prompted Tina's shift from a predominately hegemonic to oppositional femininity gender project once she entered junior high school. Tina's stepfather repeatedly assaulted her mother, who responded with passive acceptance. On numerous occasions, Tina encouraged her mother to leave him; however, her mother's fear of her husband prevented her leaving and thus the abuse continued unabated (Messerschmidt 2004, 85–86). At age twelve, Tina's increased physical strength enabled her to defend her mother from her stepfather, who eventually moved out of the house (Messerschmidt 2004, 87–88).

Shortly after Tina's stepfather moved out of the house, Tina began to exhibit more self-confidence, which she displayed through a more sexually provocative style of dress and wearing makeup (Messerschmidt 2004, 88). Tina's increased confidence and new style marks an important shift from a preppy hegemonic to bad-girl oppositional femininity gender project because self-confidence and a sexualized demeanor subvert hegemonic femininity. We can speculate that the reason why Tina actively resisted hegemonic femininity is because she witnessed the physical abuse and relatively powerless position her mother occupied within the gender regime of home and the power which can accompany the use of assaultive violence. Critically, however, Tina remained nonviolent at school until a preppy girl provoked her and thus challenged her femininity.

The definitive event which prompted Tina's shift from a hegemonic to oppositional femininity gender project within the gender regime of school occurred when Tina's best friend labeled her a *whore* and Tina beat her up. As I discussed, derogatory labels can be used to stigmatize girls whose embodied social actions violate norms of dominant and hegemonic femininities. Tina rejected the appropriate feminine response of modifying her style of dress or girlfighting by drawing on the masculine resource of physical violence, thus representing a shift from hegemonic to oppositional femininity.

As a result of engaging in assaultive violence, Tina was banished from the preppy group and recruited by the badass group (Messerschmidt 2004, 89). *Bad-girl* femininity is defined by a provocative style of dress, sexual confidence, drug and alcohol use, and physically fighting with other girls, so Tina's embodied social actions aligned with this form of femininity. Notably, badass boys and girls both participate in physical fighting, although participation in crime remains an exclusively masculine endeavor.

At first glance, gender relations appear more egalitarian within the badass group because both boys and girls participate in physical violence. However, physical fights occur exclusively among members of the same sex. For this reason, physical violence is not gendered masculine behavior within this group, but an embodied social action which concomitantly transcends gender but reinforces gender differences. Therefore, girls can engage in same-sex fighting and still remain accountably feminine. Kelly, whom I discussed in chapter 1, was a notable exception because she was awarded honorary male status and therefore permitted to fight with boys; however, while she was regarded as *unfeminine*, she was not conceptualized as *unfemale* (Messerschmidt 2004, 143). Significantly, the male group members reinforced unequal gender relations within the gang by using Kelly's sex category membership to disqualify her from participation in harder forms of crime such as burglaries and robberies, which were crucial masculine resources for individuals attempting to embody hegemonic masculinity. For this reason, gender relations within the gang cannot be characterized as egalitarian but instead as fundamentally patriarchal.

Tina's life-history interview demonstrates how the accomplishment of gender and social class co-occur within specific social contexts. Therefore, physical violence and emphasized sexuality are legitimized embodied social actions which constitute bad-girl, but not preppy, femininity. However, girls' subordinate position within both groups demonstrates how unequal gender relations can transcend other factors such as social class.

The above discussion has indicated that Tina can be conceptualized as embodying a subordinate oppositional femininity within the gender regime of the school. Although Tina's slim body conformed to the standards of dominant femininity, her provocative style of dress, emphasized sexuality, overconfident, aggressive demeanor, and violent behavior located her as gender deviant and thus subordinate in relation to hegemonic femininity. Tina's friend, who embodied preppy hegemonic femininity, subordinated Tina through the use of the label *whore*, thus creating a distance from Tina and confirming her own hegemonic femininity. Epithets such as *whore* and *slut* are policing devices girls use to sanction overconfident or assertive girls. Simultaneously, Tina constructed an oppositional femininity gender identity by engaging in the above-mentioned gender practices which subverted preppy hegemonic femininity due to their association with hegemonic masculinity. Hence, Tina's embodied social actions challenged an assumption that permissive sexuality, confidence, aggression, and physical violence are masculine gendered actions. Although Tina's embodied social actions challenged the ascendancy of preppy hegemonic masculinity, she did not contribute to equalizing gender relations, but instead embodied a subordinate oppositional femininity which reified toxic masculine qualities such as violence and aggression.

Classroom Culture of Schools

The classroom is another arena of school life where dominant, hegemonic, subordinate, and oppositional masculinities and femininities are constructed and sustained. The classroom can be seen as a public context similar to the workplace. Paralleling how accomplishment in the public context of work is defined by masculine characteristics such as competitiveness and aggressiveness, success in the classroom also involves displays of verbal bravado to compete with others. These characteristics directly oppose feminine ones, so women can face a double bind where success is accessible through characteristics which contradict dominant femininity. As a result, girls' access route to success involves practicing aspects of hegemonic masculinity and accordingly an oppositional form of femininity.

The research of Judith Baxter provides insight into the double bind that ambitious girls face when they step outside the confines of dominant femininity. Baxter (2003) conducted an investigation and analysis of the leadership styles of a class of high school students. This group of students was preparing for the General Certificate of Secondary Education (GCSE) in English, a standardized examination which measures speaking and listening ability. Baxter (2003, 82) noted a shift in the examination's assessment criteria from a focus on the ability to speak in collaborative groups to an emphasis on an individual's ability to talk in public contexts. According to the new standards, the ability to confidently articulate an opinion in front of an audience constitutes criteria for an A grade on this examination.

We can view the change in examination criteria as a shift from a stereotypically feminine speech style, which emphasizes collaboration, to a stereotypically masculine style, which foregrounds autonomy (Holmes 2006, 6). In applying the terms *masculine* and *feminine*, I am not advocating support for an essentialist claim that biological sex predetermines gendered speech style. Rather, masculine and feminine index culturally constructed embodied social actions which constitute masculinity and femininity, but are not determined by sex. Therefore, men and women can and do draw on both speech styles; however, women may face stigmatization for usurping a masculine style and transgressing femininity (Baxter 2003, 184–85; 2008, 201; Holmes 2006, 34–35).

Baxter found that teachers and students both viewed many aspects of classroom life through a lens of *gender differences*. To reflect this, Baxter (2003, 92) identified and named a discourse of *gender differentiation* or "a conventionalized set of ways of differentiating individuals' identities in the world primarily according to their sex or gender." Similar to my previous discussion of gender differences, gender differentiation is problematic because it not only attributes gendered behavior to biological sex and thus promulgates gendered stereotypes but also because it conflates effective leadership with masculinity. Therefore, the classroom teacher accepted and reinforced the popular stereotype that boys are more active than girls by allowing a boy to speak out of turn and thus violate classroom interaction rules (Baxter 2003, 105). More strikingly, however, the examination criteria constituting effective speech reflect the masculine characteristic of confident self-expression (Holmes 2006, 34; Messerschmidt 2000, 10). Not only does a discourse of gender differentiation permit boys to violate classroom interactional rituals, but displaying confidence in front of a group also wins points on the examination. Therefore, a sexual double standard exists where masculine characteristics such as confidence and verbal bravado support boys' success on this examination while girls who adopt a masculine leadership style are seen as violating norms of dominant femininity.

Women who attempt to claim and exercise power can be seen as facing a *double bind* (see Holmes 2006, 34–35) because power is associated with masculinity which by definition opposes femininity. As previously argued, feminine embodied social actions are usually assigned to individuals possessing female sex category membership, so individual behavior is often assessed according to sex category incumbency (West and Zimmerman 1987, 136). Although women may incur a certain degree of power from practicing elements of masculinity, they can also face marginalization resulting from a misalignment between sex category and embodied gendered actions.

Sophie: Subordinate Oppositional Femininity

Sophie, a student in Baxter's study, exemplifies the classic double bind that women in leadership positions face. During a collaborative group work activity, Sophie displayed characteristics associated with a masculine speech style, such as speaking for extended amounts of time, overlapping with other speakers, and directly expressing her opinion (Baxter 2006, 165). According to Baxter's observations, the other members of this all-female group appeared unoffended by Sophie's behavior during the class activity. However, students expressed a certain amount of dissent toward Sophie during post-activity individual interviews with Baxter. For example, one student referred to Sophie as a *bitch* for attempting to persuade them to accept her opinion. Notably, Sophie's marginalization by members of this group supports Brown's (2003) finding that overconfident girls can face pejorative labels.

Sophie's marginalization reflects the sometimes repressive nature of norms which constitute dominant forms of femininity. Baxter (2006, 168) convincingly argues that Sophie's masculine leadership style may be the source of her marginalization by the group. Although a confrontational communicative style is unmarked in boys, girls face social marginalization for exhibiting the same behavior (Baxter 2006, 169). In addition, we can view the other girls' reluctance to aggressively disagree with Sophie as an internalization of norms constituting dominant femininity. Instead of contesting Sophie's proposals or leadership during the activity, they engaged in girlfighting through gossiping, forming a covert alliance against Sophie, and potentially socially ostracizing her.

Sophie can be seen as embodying a subordinate oppositional femininity within the local context of this secondary school. Sophie's exhibited overconfidence marked her as an anomaly for transgressing the boundaries of dominant femininity and thus she was the target of relational aggression. Although Sophie's peers maintained a façade of niceness during the classroom activity, they indicated discontent toward Sophie's confidence during the interviews. I contend with Baxter (2006, 168–69) that Sophie faced marginalization because leadership in public contexts is usually gendered masculine, so her peers were uncomfortable with a strong female leader. The fear of gender transgression and social marginalization is one potential explanation to account for why female leaders face difficulty asserting their authority later in life (Baxter 2006, 176). Conceivably, Sophie's subordination materialized as social exclusion and occurred in venues outside the classroom, such as in the lunchroom, gymnasium, or hallways. Hence, Sophie opposed a norm that women are not self-confident speakers and more significantly contested the dominant position of masculinity and subordinate position of femininity within the classroom context.

The more far-reaching implications of Baxter's study are that assessment criteria for the GCSE posit an authoritative and thus masculine leadership style as constituting a top grade (Baxter 2006, 161). The formal authorization of a masculine discourse style on this examination's assessment criteria is disturbing as it is disadvantageous to both boys and girls who do not conform to this style and contributes to the normalization of masculine characteristics as indexing success in public contexts.

Research has demonstrated that successful leadership involves a dynamic combination of masculine and feminine leadership styles which depends upon and thus varies by workplace context (Holmes 2006, 1). In a masculinized workplace culture, exemplified by large corporations, a more authoritarian leadership style may constitute successful leadership. On the other hand, in a femininzed workplace culture, characteristic of smaller organizations, a more collaborative approach may constitute effective leadership. Since gender is not static, masculine and feminine are not rigid categorizations but always a matter of degree, contextually variant, and subject to change. For instance, contemporary workplaces may embrace a more progressive management philosophy that privileges egalitarian relationships through teamwork and shared decision making. Therefore, if a major goal of education is to prepare students for participation in the paid labor force, then the GCSE's exclusive validation of an authoritarian leadership style does not prepare students for success in a variety of workplace contexts.

Gender Relations in School

The preceding discussion of the construction of gender within the gender regimes of schools has implications for each of the four dimensions of gender relations. Striking parallels can be drawn between the social organization of schools and that of other social institutions, such as the family and workplace. Therefore, dominant forms of femininity and masculinity are constructed and maintained within schools and form the basis for the organization of gender regimes in other areas of society.

Power Relations

Power relations were reflected in the unequal social organization of the school. Girls' unrecognized supportive work as organizers of social events and cheerleaders was crucial for the success of these events and forming the school's overall social climate. School-based gender relations relegate women to supportive positions which perform important social functions but lack institutional authority. Therefore, their backstage, supportive work was largely unnoticed and underappreciated. Similarly, girls' underrepresentation in positions with institutional authority such as class president and star athlete reflects the saturation of women in low status positions within the workplace (Connell 2009, 117–18; Lorber 1994, 228) and thereby mirrors the relationship between hegemonic masculinity and hegemonic femininity.

Non-egalitarian power relations were reflected in athletics. While athletic prowess enhances a boy's masculinity, women athletes face a double bind where their participation in sports potentially compromises their femininity, so they have to expend additional effort emphasizing their heterofemininity or else face derogatory labels. In reference to cheerleading, Adams and Bettis (2003, 57) point out how collegiate cheerleaders are not awarded scholarships and coaches' salaries are lower than other sports. These sexist practices are further indicators that women's sports are awarded less prestige than men's sports and also reflect unequal power relations.

Unequal power relations were also reflected within the classroom. A discourse of gender differentiation positioned effective leadership as masculine. As a result, girls face a dilemma because their feminine accountability disqualifies them for leadership positions. This dilemma or double bind was exemplified by Sophie, who performed leadership through usurping a masculine leadership style and was marginalized by her peers. The disempowering nature of the double bind and strategies that female leaders use to resolve it are further discussed in chapter 3.

Production Relations

The social organization of both the school and classroom cultures reflected production relations. Female students performed the behind-the-scenes, essential work of organizing social events and providing support at athletic events which supported the overall social climate of the school and ultimately the ascendance of hegemonic masculinity. Much like the undervalued, yet essential, domestic labor of love women have traditionally performed for their families, boys' success in public roles in athletics and student government is arguably contingent upon females' support. Indeed, girls' support through fundraising, organizing social events, and cheerleading forms the backbone of the social climate of the school and allows boys to focus solely on cultivating a public persona.

A division of labor also emerged within the classroom where boys dominated class discussions and girls were denied access to the floor. This unequal division of discursive labor was supported by both the girls and teacher. The boys frequently violated classroom rules by speaking out of turn and interrupting other students while the girls observed the classroom rules of not speaking out of turn or interrupting others. The teacher encouraged the boys' dominance of the classroom floor by permitting them to violate the classroom rules and indirectly contributed to silencing the girls. Paralleling the division of labor outside of the classroom, girls supported the boys' dominance of public spaces and contributed to their own oppression.

Emotional Relations

Unsurprisingly, heteronormative gender relations formed the foundation of emotional relations within the gender regime of high school. The emergent heterosexual market, where heterosexuality is the only legitimized sexuality, demonstrates the hegemonic status of heterosexuality and subordinated status of alternative sexualities within the gender regimes of schools. Schools actively participate in the process of sanctioning heterosexuality by selecting a prom king and queen, publishing yearbook pictures of the *best* or *cutest* couple, adopting a heteronormative sex education curriculum, and ignoring homophobic comments (see Pascoe 2007).

We also saw emotional relations come into play in the type of work students performed. Boys monopolized the masculine arenas of student government and certain athletics while girls dominated the more feminized spaces of social committees, theater, and feminine sports such as cheerleading. Lorber (1994, 226) makes the conspicuous point that women are seen as legitimate leaders in certain areas such as health, education, and welfare but not in the top echelons of business and politics. Clearly, women are seen as bona fide leaders in professions which emphasize caregiving and consequently are undervalued due to their association with the home and femininity. The result of men's disinterest in assuming authoritative positions within these professions is that women have been allowed to assume leadership positions; however, employment in these feminine professions does not incur equivalent financial remuneration and social prestige. Similarly, girls can occupy leadership positions on social committees and cheerleading squads, which do not threaten male power, but not within the classroom, as the case of Sophie demonstrated.

Symbolic Relations

Symbolic relations were reflected in the idealization of thinness, youth, and sexual appeal. As a girl's popularity is contingent upon entering into a heterosexual relationship with a popular boy, her physical appearance and sexual appeal are essential feminine resources for securing a relationship. Therefore, girls may attempt to enhance their attractiveness through cosmetics, fashion, and stringent dieting regimes. The importance of a woman's appearance was also reflected in verbal insults and fat talk, which girls used to enforce same-sex hierarchies and compete for boys' attention. Finally, we saw how sexuality discourses construct a virgin/whore dichotomy and thus girls must be careful to avoid the appearance of promiscuity. To be labeled a slut would result in a decline in value on the heterosexual market. These examples illustrate how symbolically constructed notions of femininity, which are promoted by the media and popular culture, can influence the material practices of actual girls.

Oppositional Femininities' Role in Troubling Gender Relations

Oppositional femininities demonstrate how individuals possess agency to threaten the hierarchical and complementary relationship definitive of hegemonic masculinity and hegemonic femininity and potentially reconstitute hegemonic gender relations. Indeed, oppositional femininities by definition contest unequal gender relations as they refuse to form a complementary, compliant relationship with hegemonic masculinity. Despite their subversive potential, it is necessary to distinguish between oppositional femininities whose power stems solely from association with hegemonic masculinity from those who challenge the exalted status of hegemonic masculine characteristics and thus contribute to transforming a patriarchal gender order.

Power accompanies the use of violence due to its association with hegemonic masculinity. However, violence can be both a tool utilized to claim power over others and a defense mechanism available for protection. For this reason, we need to critically scrutinize the reasons why Tina used the masculine resource of violence and disentangle the subversive from oppressive elements of violence.

Tina engaged in assaultive violence to serve two different purposes. First, she engaged in protective violence to destabilize masculine dominance and control within the home (Messerschmidt 2004, 120). Tina witnessed the brutal effects of domestic violence and the ineffectiveness of the legitimated feminine response of verbal negotiation. Indeed, Tina initially appealed to her stepfather to stop the abuse, but this nonviolent method was apparently ineffective as the violence continued unabated. Accordingly, we can positively conceptualize Tina's use of physical force against her stepfather because it was not utilized to subordinate others and thus destructive, but rather it was a protective response to violence directed at a loved one and potential insurance against future attacks. As a result, Tina quickly learned that the normalized masculine response of physical retaliation can terminate abuse and intimidate others.

Second, Tina used physical violence to construct and assert her school-based bad-girl femininity persona. Similar to how men use violence against others to construct and reaffirm their masculinity, Tina used violence against preppy girls who verbally challenged her femininity and in the process reconfirmed her bad-girl femininity. Tina challenged preppy hegemonic femininity by adopting a sexualized demeanor and using direct versus relational aggression; nevertheless, she reaffirmed the use of violence as a legitimated response to verbal abuse. Thus, her embodied social actions align with those of boys and men who use violence as a restorative device for their injured masculine pride.

Although Tina drew on physical violence to protect her mother, which challenges the assumption that women passively and undisputedly submit to men's authority, she ultimately utilized violence to intimidate preppy girls and construct a violent bad-girl femininity gender project. In the end, Tina's embodied social actions reaffirm the principle that physical force is a legitimated response to femininity (or masculinity) challenges and contributed to sustaining an oppressive masculine practice.

Tina's experience with domestic violence arguably taught her that increased power can accompany the use of assaultive violence. Indeed, Tina learned that the legitimated feminine response of verbal negotiation is ineffective compared with the masculine response of physical retaliation. As a result, Tina immediately responded with physical violence when a preppy girl challenged her femininity. Significantly, the power which accompanies the use of physical violence stems from its association with hegemonic masculinity, but women's use of violence does not contribute to equalizing gender relations. Although Tina challenged the assumption that women are nonviolent, she also contributed to sustaining an oppressive masculine practice.

Bad-girl femininity appears to contest emotional relations through the legitimization of an active female sexuality. Closer scrutiny reveals that while badass girls appear empowered by their ability to display self-confidence and assert their sexuality, the heterosexual matrix remains as the structuring agent for gender relations within the gang, and thus their sexualized demeanor is validated by and ultimately performed for a male gaze. Although emphasized female sexuality appears to dismantle the virgin/whore dichotomy, bad-girl and preppy sexuality are equally constrictive. Paralleling how preppy girls use relational aggression and conservative sexuality to construct same-sex hierarchical relationships and negotiate status, badass girls draw on physical fighting and a sexualized demeanor to compete for boys' attention and secure monogamous heterosexual relationships. Notably, a sexual double standard also infiltrates the badass group which normalizes permissive male sexuality and monogamous female sexuality. For these reasons, bad-girl femininity does not challenge heteronormativity and a cultural ideology that posits romantic relationships as a trademark element of femininity.

Although I have characterized both Sophie and Tina as subordinate oppositional femininities, the ways in which they oppose hegemonic femininity are fundamentally different, which illustrate how hegemonic, subordinate, and oppositional femininities vary by local, regional, and global contexts. Tina transgressed gender norms through her overconfidence, expressed sexuality, and complete rejection of the school culture through resisting authority. Hence, Tina embodied a subordinate oppositional femininity in the local context of the school where preppy femininity is hegemonic. Nonetheless, skipping school, nonconservative fashion, sexual relations with boys, and same-sex fighting are legitimized feminine social actions which complement and are subordinate to hegemonic masculine ones. As a result, Tina embodied a badass form of hegemonic femininity within the gender regime of the street where preppy femininity would be subordinate.

In notable contrast, Sophie challenged a norm that confident verbal expression is a masculine gender practice but accepted the school culture through conforming to school rules. Conceivably, Sophie could also embody hegemonic or dominant femininity in another school context such as an elite private school where girls and boys are expected to compete and excel academically. It needs to be underscored that dominant, hegemonic, subordinate, and oppositional femininities are unfixed, fluid constructs which exhibit local, regional, and global variation.

Crisis Tendencies

Gender nonconformists such as Sophie can promulgate the formation of crisis tendencies which serve as catalysts for the creation of more egalitarian gender relations within the gender regimes of schools. Sophie contested the assumption that girls are nonassertive leaders; however, she paid the price of social isolation from other classmates and ultimately her biological sex prevented her from commanding the same level of authority that a powerful male speaker wields. At the same time, the goal of gender equality should not be for women to conform to masculine norms, but that masculine and feminine, as far as these terms are definable, are equally valued and thus leadership de-gendered. Nevertheless, individuals such as Sophie challenge the essentialist claim that gender directly follows in the footsteps of biological sex and thus contest the assumption that successful leadership ability is restricted to men.

Discussion

The emergent gender division of school labor and cultural norms which disassociate femininity and public speaking illustrate how embodying hegemonic femininity is indeed a paradoxical privilege for girls. Defining elements of hegemonic femininity such as the privileging of physical appearance, cultivating heterosexual romance before personal ambitions, and assuming supportive versus leadership roles collectively contribute to women's overall subordination in relation to men. A significant difference between masculinity and femininity, then, is that while men are empowered by displays of power or aggression, the celebrated characteristics associated with hegemonic femininity work to subordinate and ultimately disempower women.

Another fundamental and enduring difference between masculinity and femininity is that while boys can directly gain access to the embodiment of dominant and hegemonic forms of masculinity through personal achievements, girls' gendered accomplishments are contingent upon, and thus mediated through, their successful navigation of the heterosexual market. Crucially, the heterosexual market empowers boys with the ability to select their heterosexual partners and ultimately evaluate who possesses the feminine capital signifying the successful accomplishment of heterofemininities. Similar to how some women gain a degree of social prestige not through individual accomplishments but through marriage to a successful corporate executive, girls can raise their status within the school by dating a popular athlete. However, as Eckert and McConnell-Ginet (2003, 38) insightfully point out, a married woman's social position depends upon both her husband's social position and distribution of accrued resources to her. Therefore, a girl's popularity rests on being chosen by a popular boy and his public acknowledgment of their relationship. The embodiment of hegemonic femininity involves forming nonplatonic heterosexual relationships and assuming a supportive role which may provide women with a legitimized social identity which is subordinate to hegemonic masculinity.

Conclusion

This chapter has discussed the construction of dominant, hegemonic, and subordinate oppositional femininities within the gender regimes of secondary schools. The social organization of schools reflects a traditional gendered division of labor where boys construct their masculinity through visible roles in athletics and student government and girls construct their femininity through supportive roles such as cheerleaders and organizers of social events. Although girls' supportive activities support the school's overall social climate, similar to domestic labor, they are not granted the same degree of institutional prestige and recognition as boys' activities.

My discussion of the heterosexual marketplace indicates that heterosexuality is the structuring agent of emotional relations within schools. Notably, boys' and girls' market value differs on the heterosexual market, where girls' value is contingent upon attractiveness and forming a romantic attachment with a popular boy and boys' value fluctuates based upon athletic prowess. Since ideologies of femininity forbid explicit displays of aggression, girls utilize subterranean girlfighting to ostracize other girls and compete for the attention of popular boys. An unfortunate consequence of girlfighting is that it prevents the formation of supportive alliances among girls and between girls and boys who do not subscribe to hegemonic masculinity.

The chapter also presented two case studies of gender nonconforming subordinate oppositional femininities. Tina was a working class girl who subverted middle-class preppy hegemonic femininity through adopting a sexualized demeanor and participating in violence. Tina's embodied social actions subverted constrictive aspects of preppy hegemonic femininity such as passive sexuality and subdued self-confidence and thus appear empowering. Unfortunately, her use of physical violence ultimately reconfirmed an oppressive masculine practice and thus Tina cannot be seen as contributing to transforming unequal gender relations.

Sophie was a middle-class girl who subverted hegemonic femininity through adopting a masculine leadership style during a classroom activity. Although we might consider a more facilitative, feminine leadership style as less authoritarian and therefore preferable, Sophie's style reflected the discursive norms of that specific classroom context. As I demonstrate in the next chapter, the normalization of certain leadership styles depends upon the norms of particular workplace contexts. Hence, Sophie is not merely conforming to a masculine norm, but also adjusting her leadership style to reflect the norms of the classroom context. Sophie demonstrates how individuals can adopt a leadership style regardless of gender and therefore is contributing to the de-gendering of leadership. For these reasons, Sophie contests the assumption that only men are effective leaders and can be seen as embodying an *equality femininity* who contributes to democratizing gender relations.

The subordination of gender nonconforming girls through girlfighting is one way girls police and sustain the boundaries of dominant femininity. Notably, displaying self-confidence and affirming one's heterosexuality are masculine resources which confirm masculinity while these same characteristics disconfirm femininity. By engaging in girlfighting, girls ensure that these characteristics remain men's exclusive possession and in the process sustain a hierarchical and supposedly complementary relationship between men and women, masculinity and femininity.

The next chapter concerns the challenges that professional women face as they attempt to balance the competing demands of work, home, and feminine accountability.

4

Gender and Professional Identity in the Workplace

T he first chapter discussed how a gender division of labor common in many Western countries posits women's social contribution in the private realm of the home and men's in the public realm of workplace organizations. Many notions of masculinity and femininity stem from this division of labor. For instance, culturally dominant ideologies associate femininity with caregiving, nurturing, and selflessness (Weedon 1987, 2; Wajcman 1998, 60), while leadership ability and participation in the paid labor force are analogous to masculinity (Martin and Jurik 2007, 43). It also needs to be underscored that domestic work is an unpaid, undervalued labor of love while nondomestic work results in a wage and social prestige, so culturally construed gendered labor is unequally valued. For these reasons, workplaces are arguably another site to study the construction of femininities.

The focus of this chapter is the intersection between gender and professional identity. Specifically, I discuss women working in the nontraditional occupations of law enforcement, law, corporate management, and the priesthood. In the process of identity formation, these women are confronted with the classic double bind of constructing a professional identity while remaining accountably feminine. Women who successfully construct their professional identity may simultaneously subvert norms constituting dominant femininity and inadvertently construct oppositional femininities. This chapter discusses how professional women confront and sometimes resolve the pernicious double bind through inculcating, eschewing, or reformulating dominant femininities.

Gendered Division of Labor

Women's increased participation in the paid workforce has promulgated the amelioration, but not total abolition, of the gender division of labor. Indeed, working women are confronted with balancing the sometimes conflicting demands of professional responsibilities and *second shift* of housework and childcare duties, which approximates an extra month of twenty-four-hour days per annum (Hochschild 1989, 3–4). Families with sufficient financial resources can reduce the second shift through purchasing additional household labor; however, women remain responsible for the coordination of the execution and management of these services—thus the second shift may be reduced but it is not completely eliminated (Bagilhole 2002, 92; Pyke 1996, 553; Wacjman 1998, 152).

The expectation that women manage most aspects of domestic life is also reflected in corporate policies which attest to the *family-friendly* nature of the workplaces. Although many organizations articulate this seemingly gender-neutral rhetoric, the fact remains that women perform the majority of household labor and therefore *mother-friendly* more accurately describes such policies (Wacjman 1998, 26). The gendering of parenting is highly problematic because it not only releases men from domestic involvement but also over-burdens women. Consequently, women's careers are ascribed secondary status to men's and their career advancement is severely inhibited.

One consequence of an asymmetrical division of labor is that husbands' careers take precedence over their wives'. Pyke (1996, 533) refers to this oppressive phenomenon as the *hegemony of the male career*. The logic of this pervasive ideology is that a husband's breadwinner role and accompanying professional responsibilities entail long work hours which in turn prevent him from making a substantial domestic contribution. Clearly this ideology disadvantages professional women by failing to ascribe equal value to their careers.

The insidious nature of this ideology makes it appear gender-neutral, when in fact it obscures gendered power relations and contributes to women's subordination. It can be argued that if a wife is the main family breadwinner, then her career would take precedence over her husband's and release her from performing domestic work. Despite the appeal of such a gender-neutral explanation, cultural ideologies of femininity and masculinity differently position individuals' relationship to the home and workplace. As I previously discussed, an omnipresent cultural ideology exists which maintains that women mother and manage the household regardless of their occupational status (Bagilhole 2002, 135; Pyke 1996, 533; Wacjman 1998, 26). For this reason, it is highly unlikely that women's careers will achieve hegemonic status. The examination of other social classes provides support for this argument.

For instance, working-class households often depend upon a dual income; however, this situation does not result in a more egalitarian distribution of domestic labor. Unlike higher-class men, working-class men cannot rely on their career responsibilities and sole breadwinner status as the basis for their entitlement to domestic noninvolvement, so they depend upon patriarchal ideologies (Pyke 1996, 540–41). As a result, women from various social classes are confronted with the ubiquitous second shift.

In addition to the hegemony of a male career, another consequence of an unequal division of labor is that men's career trajectories are also hegemonic. An *ideal worker's* (Williams 2000, 1) career path is characterized by long hours, geographic mobility, and continuous employment, unencumbered by domestic responsibilities, which presumes a wife's domestic support and is therefore gendered masculine (Bagilhole 2002, 99; Lorber 1994, 197; Stone 2008, 82–83; Wajcman 1998, 26). The necessity of taking maternity leave, men's reluctance to utilize childcare leave, and cultural assumption that women manage the household collectively disadvantage professional women.

Occupational Gendered Divisions of Labor

Gendered divisions of labor not only emerge as a bifurcation between domestic and nondomestic labor, but also as the gendering of certain professions and specializations within those occupations. A *horizontal gender division of labor* (Burr 1998, 5) refers to how men and women are considered predisposed to work in certain professions due to the naturalization of gender differences discourses. For instance, elementary school teaching, nursing, and social work are gendered as feminine, while business and educational administration, law, and medicine are considered masculine (Lorber 1994, 210). Gender divisions of labor also emerge among specialties within professions or *vertical segregation* (Wajcman 1998, 48). Vertical segregation is exemplified in masculine professions such as medicine and law, where men specialize in more prestigious, hospital-based specialties or litigation and women in primary care and family law (Lorber 1994, 198; Pierce 1995, 30). Even in traditionally feminine occupations such as nursing, men are channeled into better paying administrative and leadership positions while women remain as nurses (Williams 1989, 9). Paralleling how domestic work is an underappreciated labor of love, both feminine professions and feminine specializations within professions are underpaid and undervalued (Lorber 1994, 196–97), thereby reflecting the overall cultural devaluation of femininity.

The patterns of gender practice which underpin gender divisions of labor substantiate a complementary and hierarchical relationship between men and women, masculinity and femininity and thereby constitute gender hegemony.

Hegemonic femininity is associated with unpaid domestic labor or combining domestic and nondomestic work. As a domestic homemaker receives no wage, she is financially dependent on, and thus subordinate to, a male bread-winner. A *superwoman* who faces the double burden of domestic and nondomestic work is clearly disadvantaged and subordinate to a man who can direct most of his attention to his career. In contrast to hegemonic femininity, hegemonic masculinity is associated with paid nondomestic labor where men accrue social prestige, power, and material wealth. Workplace-internal divisions of labor are underpinned by ideologies of masculinity and femininity which construe men as natural leaders and women as supporters. Therefore, the gendered characteristics of caregiving versus providing, administrating versus facilitating, create and sustain an unequal relationship between men and women, masculinity and femininity, and illustrate gender hegemony.

The next section concerns women employed in stereotypically masculine professions who contest the hierarchical relationship definitive of masculinity and femininity and thus can be seen as oppositional femininities.

Nontraditional Occupations

Nontraditional occupations "denote any occupation which is, or has been, traditionally undertaken by a man" (Bagilhole 2002, 3). Examples include law, police work, corporate management, and the priesthood. These professions are arguably a suitable site to study the construction of hegemonic and oppositional femininities because their status as exclusive masculine terrain makes them particularly reluctant to accept women and assign them full professional status. Hence, women face a double bind due to the tension between constructing a professional identity and remaining accountably feminine. The double bind is particularly salient concerning gender-variant expectations for the performance of emotional labor.

The Gendered Division of Emotional Labor

Arlie Hochschild (1983) maintains that occupations require the performance of certain types of emotional labor. The performance of *emotional labor* requires workers "to induce or suppress feeling in order to sustain the outward countenance that produces the proper state of mind in others" (Hochschild 1983, 3). In Hochschild's (1983, 137–47) study, flight attendants were expected to suppress feelings of irritation and continually inflate their customers' status, while bill collectors strategically deployed negative affect in order to deflate their clients' status. The concept of emotional labor demonstrates how emotion, which is typically associated with the private realm and femininity, has become commercialized in the public sector and essential for the successful performance of professional identity.

Although the *commercialization of human feeling* blurs the public/private divide, men and women are held accountable to produce different types of emotional labor, which indicates that it is gendered. Hochschild skillfully demonstrates how certain occupations such as flight attendants and bill collectors are inherently gendered and thus require the production of feminine and masculine emotional labor. In addition, regardless of the occupation, men and women are expected to perform different emotional labor, which indicates the omnirelevance of sex category as the main determinant for ascribing gendered accountability. For example, Pierce (1995, 147) demonstrated how male paralegals were allowed to display affective neutrality or politeness, while female paralegals were expected to exhibit deference and caretaking. Noticeably, regardless of the association between paralegals and femininity, men were still held accountable to masculinity and thus expected to display masculinized emotional labor. Seemingly, sex category membership overrides the gendered nature of an occupation as the main determinant for ascribing expectations regarding the performance of emotional labor.

The next section focuses on the workplace cultures and normative forms of emotional labor in the nontraditional professions of police work, law, corporate management, and the priesthood.

Emotional Labor in Nontraditional Occupations

The emotional labor expected of employees in nontraditional occupations can be glossed masculine. However, I will demonstrate how individuals working in these professions uniquely combine masculine and feminine forms of emotional labor, which underscores how a masculine/feminine dichotomy is oversimplistic and fails to capture the dynamic nature of professional identity construction. Significantly, however, men and women working in these professions are held to nonreciprocal norms: women are expected to perform more feminized and men more masculinized emotional labor. These expectations demonstrate the entrenched nature of the association between sex category membership and gendered accountability. Despite the fact that men working in these professions perform both masculine and feminine emotional labor, women remain accountable to femininity. Overcoming men's continuous accentuation of women's femininity and thus unsuitability for these occupations can be conceptualized as one of the major challenges facing professional women who attempt to resolve the double bind of claiming professional status as women.

Prior to discussing the specific types of emotional labor expected of ideal employees in these nontraditional occupations, it is first necessary to discuss how the masculinized workplace cultures of these professions impact the performance of gendered professional identities. Since men, who are accountable to masculinity, have traditionally dominated these professions, a homosocial, masculine workplace culture prevails (Bagilhole 2002, 116–18, 184; Wajcman 1998, 52). Homosociality refers to "the bonding of men of the same race, religion, and social-class background" (Lorber 1994, 231). Men tend to form *old-boy networks* through professional organization membership, work-based and after-hours socialization, and the formation of intermale alliances (Bagilhole 2002, 118–19; Martin and Jurik 2007, 113–14; Pierce 1995, 106; Wajcman 1998, 52–53).

Through the development of and participation in this masculinist work culture, men construct *affiliating masculinities* which "involve relating to, or connecting with, rather than distancing, or separating, from others" (Martin 2001, 604). The benefits they incur from constructing and enacting affiliating masculinities include access to important information, opportunities to develop and expand professional networks, and the inside track to career advancement. Women who actively contest this component of work culture through, for example, eating lunch at their desks or not engaging in small talk find that this resistance can curtail their promotion opportunities (Martin 2001, 596; Martin and Jurik 2007, 145).

Although some women actively resist and thus contribute to their own exclusion from the homosocial work culture, women who attempt to penetrate this impervious all-male enclave may face resistance from men. Indeed, men consciously engage in *boundary heightening*, which involves accentuating gender differences through making sexist remarks, intentionally selecting stereotypical masculine conversational topics to exclude women, and turning social events into informal competitions (Bagilhole 2002, 123; Martin and Jurik 2007, 113–14; Pierce 1995, 106–7; Wajcman 1998, 52–53).

A crucial difference between professional men and women is that while the workplace remains a primary site where men concomitantly construct their masculine and professional identities, it is not a key site to accomplish femininity. The firm association between paid labor and masculinity, conflation of masculinity with authority, masculinist workplace culture, and boundary heightening collectively contribute to exclude women and undermine any association between femininity and professional success. Therefore, women face a no-win situation where those who conform to the quintessentially masculinist workplace culture are stigmatized as gender deviants, while those who embrace or emphasize their femininity are regarded as failed career professionals (Martin and Jurik 2007, 47; Pierce 1995, 113–17; Wajcman 1998, 111). In order to resolve the double bind, women mobilize unique strategies of accommodation, subversion, and reformulation of gendered norms as they construct their professional identities.

The next section first focuses on normative expectations regarding the display of emotional labor for male employees within these professions. Then I discuss how women resolve the dilemma posed by the incompatibility between gendered accountability and professional success.

Emotional Labor in Law Enforcement

Crime fighting is the aspect of police work which has resulted in the profession being regarded as masculine and therefore suitable for men (Martin and Jurik 2007, 61). While fighting crime is one aspect of law enforcement, more common components of the job include responding to calls and emergencies, traffic enforcement, and substantial report writing (Martin and Jurik 2007, 61). The type of masculine emotional labor required to successfully combat crime involves aggressiveness, courage, and toughness, but responding to distress calls and interacting with victims requires different types of emotional labor. The strong association between police work and crime fighting downplays the more mundane, but equally important, aspects of this profession which do not require the use of physical force or aggression.

McElhinny (1995, 220) contends that the bureaucratization of the police force has promulgated a shift in norms constituting emotional labor. Far from entailing the use of physical aggression, police officers are expected to exhibit composure, objectivity, and emotional detachment. The traumatic and dangerous nature of police work suggests that the ability to create an emotional distance from these highly stressful and emotionally charged situations is crucial to preserve one's psychological health and avoid professional burnout.

McElhinny (1995, 228) applies the term *economy of affect* to describe the requisite emotional labor for police work. It logically follows that since police work is emotionally draining, officers need to conserve this scarce commodity or else it could become unavailable and result in their inability to adequately perform the job. Consequently, police officers only parcel out this sparse commodity when absolutely necessary and in many situations adopt a brusque, businesslike demeanor (McElhinny 1995, 228).

McElhinny (1995, 238) convincingly argues that a shift in police officer masculinity is occurring from a more working-class masculinity (which privileges physical and emotional aggression) toward a more middle-class masculinity (which foregrounds nonaggression and emotional restraint). Nevertheless, since rationality and emotional control are masculine attributes, we can conceptualize these shifting values as signifying a remasculinization, not feminization, of the police force. Noticeably, mutual group membership as a police officer superseded sex category membership as the overriding factor which influenced the performance of emotional labor. McElhinny's study demonstrates how shared group membership and the institutional norms which constitute that affiliation can transcend gender and result in similar behavior.

The preceding discussion of emotional labor in the police force has implications for the relationship between femininity and masculinity. As McElhinny's research demonstrated, a shift is occurring regarding the requisite emotional labor for performing police work from a working to middle-class form of masculinity. Currently, rational, objective, and unemotional are definitive features of the profession. Arguably, these characteristics are not merely desirable but also superior to stereotypical feminine ones such as personal, discretionary, and emotional. Thus, police officers are expected to deliver a type of emotional that is associated with a middle-class form of hegemonic masculinity and is superior to both nonhegemonic masculinities and femininities. Although seemingly less repressive than working-class characteristics of physical force and emotional aggression, the fact remains that masculine characteristics are still the sine qua non of professional success, therein substantiating asymmetrical gender relations and producing a state of gender hegemony. As Connell and Messerschmidt (2005, 852) and Messerschmidt (2010, 44–45) point out, "masculinities are configurations of practice that are constructed, unfold, and change over time." The implications of this statement are that masculinities can reconfigure into new patterns of practice which reestablish gender hegemony or equalize gender relations.

Despite the changing nature of institutional norms which govern police work, the profession remains strongly gendered masculine (Martin and Jurik 2007, 67; McElhinny 1995, 238). As a result, women can still face a double bind posed by the supposed incompatibility of their sex category and occupational identity as they attempt to assert their institutional authority and perform their professional identities. In order to resolve this dilemma, women devise unique strategies.

Susan Ehrlich Martin and Nancy Jurik (2007) have identified some strategies that women police officers use to resolve the double bind posed by their gendered accountability and professional identities. POLICEwomen refer to those who attempt to negotiate their occupational identities through disassociating from femininity and practicing masculinity (Martin and Jurik 2007, 100). These individuals aim for full acceptance as *one of the boys*, which they attempt to accomplish through displaying aggression and macho behavior. In the process of attempting to embody masculinity, their subversion of femininity results in stigmatizing labels such as *dyke* or *bitch* (Martin and Jurik 2007, 100). These disparaging epithets illustrate how nonnormative gendered performances are typically sanctioned (West and Zimmerman 1987, 136).

PoliceWOMEN, by contrast, are uncomfortable with the more dangerous aspects of law enforcement and seek non-patrol assignments (Martin and Jurik 2007, 101). They confirm feminine stereotypes through their reluctance to assume control of situations and assert their authority. Indubitably, this strategy reaffirms women's unsuitability for police work and undermines the progress made by women who have demonstrated their professional competence.

Still other women choose to strike a balance between the two aforementioned strategies. These women do not attempt to pass as one of the boys but instead project a professional image, utilize a team approach, and use humor to build camaraderie and circumvent sexual advances of colleagues (Martin and Jurik 2007, 102). Through the simultaneous adoption and adaptation of professional norms, these women can be seen as contributing to changing the masculine nature of police work.

The preceding discussion has indicated a shift in police masculinity from working-class to middle-class professional values and emotional labor. Significantly, professional norms, not gender, are the overriding factor influencing the production of emotional labor, and thus women and men are equally capable of successfully performing the job. Notwithstanding, the strategies women police officers employed to perform their professional identities suggests the superiority of masculine emotional labor is a gendered practice which is utilized to legitimize an unequal relationship between men and women, masculinity and femininity. Due to sex category membership, women are viewed as unsuitable to perform aspects of the job. As a result, some women appropriated an overcompensatory POLICEwomen strategy and in the process constructed an oppositional femininity identity which contested unequal gender relations. Simultaneously, however, this strategy contributed to the exaltation of hegemonic masculine emotional labor and denigration of femininity. Although these women may accrue a degree of power and authority through appropriating a masculine gender practice, they also risk stigmatization and marginalization for their eschewal of femininity. In contrast, women who adopted a policeWOMEN strategy formed a complementary and unequal relationship with hegemonic masculinity and thus contributed to reifying the association between men and patrol work and women with supportive non-patrol work. Finally, women who combined masculine and feminine forms of emotional labor contributed to de-gendering this aspect of the profession and potentially equalizing gender relations.

Women police officers are not the only professionals who face a double bind due to the supposed incompatibility between femininity and the masculinized emotional labor requirements of the profession. Women lawyers also devise unique strategies as they attempt to resolve this inevitable and pervasive dilemma.

Emotional Labor in the Legal Profession

Litigation is a strongly masculinized legal specialization due to its association with aggression, intimidation, and toughness (Martin and Jurik 2007, 130; Pierce 1995, 2). Gendered metaphors of a masculine *Rambo litigator* and counterpart feminine *mothering paralegal* continue to circulate and constitute idealized norms for these professions. Notions of gender appropriate emotional labor stem from these metaphors and constitute normative expectations for individuals working in these professions.

Pierce (1995) conducted a study of a law firm and corporate legal department and found that male lawyers displayed two types of *gamesmanship* or emotional labor (Pierce 1995, 23). Aggression and intimidation constitute one component of gamesmanship while strategic friendliness, or the use of charm and flattery, is another less publicized form of emotional labor that attorneys frequently employ (Pierce 1995, 51–52). The common thread which links these two apparently polarized forms of emotional labor is that they share the common instrumental goal of defeating one's opponent and winning a case.

Unlike police officers, who conserve their scarce emotional reserves, successful litigation depends upon the uneconomical expenditure of institutionally sanctioned emotional labor. Lawyers not only employ the stereotypically masculine adversarial emotional labor of aggression and intimidation, but also the more cultivated emotional labor of utilizing cajolement, friendliness, and politeness in order to strategically exploit the witnesses and create a favorable impression with the jury (Pierce 1995, 58, 72). Notably, both types of emotional labor are strongly manipulative, fiercely competitive, and share the objective of crushing one's opponent, thus exemplifying a masculine style of emotional labor. For this reason, women litigators must overcome the hurdle posed by their sex category membership and desire to be seen as professionally competent.

The gendered metaphors of Rambo litigator and mothering paralegal and requisite emotional labor for each profession establish and maintain a hierarchical and complementary relationship between masculinity and femininity and thereby constitute a state of gender hegemony. In this context, we can view litigators and the emotional labor of *gamesmanship* as constituting hegemonic masculinity. Mothering paralegals and the emotional labor of deference and caretaking exemplify hegemonic femininity, which accommodates and is subordinate to hegemonic masculinity. Due to a fundamental incompatibility between sex category membership and professional accountability, women lawyers have to devise unique strategies as they negotiate a professional identity.

Similar to police officers, women attorneys developed distinctive strategies which reproduced, destabilized, and sometimes redefined masculinized emotional labor. There was a common tendency among women to reject the adversarial model and adopt a more caring orientation in social interaction (Pierce 1995, 104). This is not to suggest that women are inherently more relationship-oriented than men, but that gendered norms constituting femininity construct women as caregivers. Women lawyers simultaneously engaged with the masculine norms governing the profession and the gendered constraints posed by femininity as they dynamically constructed their professional identities (Pierce 1995, 105).

Pierce (1995, 121) termed one strategy *resisting and reshaping the adversarial role*. Women who used this strategy rejected the adversarial model and instead attempted to form more egalitarian professional relationships with clients, colleagues, support staff, and even opposing counsel. For example, some lawyers indicated that they resolved legal disputes without the use of confrontational tactics and respected secretaries' opinions. These women can be seen as rejecting the masculine adversarial style and redefining the legal profession based on the principles of trust, mutual respect, and amicable resolution.

Another strategy, *splitting the roles versus distancing* involves (Pierce 1995, 127) assimilating to the combative litigator model when dealing with clients and opposing counsel, but adopting a more civilized approach when interacting with colleagues and support staff. For instance, one lawyer was confrontational and used aggressive tactics when dealing with opposing counsel, but was pleasant and attentive to clerical staff. This strategy exemplifies both the firm connection between masculinized gamesmanship and professional success and the fundamental tension between feminized emotional labor and success. Although these women reject the adversarial model outside the courtroom, they appropriate it for instrumental means and thereby contribute to the reaffirmation of this masculine strategy and its conflation with professional success.

The final strategy—*talk like a lawyer, think like a lawyer, act like a lawyer*— refers to women who uncompromisingly conform to the adversarial style (Pierce 1995, 132). In addition to using aggressive tactics in the courtroom, these women formed professional working relationships with their support staff but did not attempt to reduce status boundaries or build friendships with them. Problematically, women who utilize this strategy inadvertently contribute to the normalization of a masculine style as definitive of professional success. Indeed, the adversarial masculine style becomes the gold standard that everyone should aspire to emulate, and the potential for a diverse range of

professional styles to receive validation is reduced. As Lorber (1994) insightfully points out, "equality does not mean sameness or even similarity; it
means that different talents and contributions are equally valued and rewarded" (294). Regarding the legal profession, a masculine style is clearly
construed as superordinate and alternative styles rendered subordinate, reflecting the hierarchical and complementary relationship of hegemonic masculinity and hegemonic femininity.

Paralleling my discussion of women police officers' gender strategies to
perform their professional identities, women litigators' strategies also have
implications for the relationship between masculinity and femininity. As I
have already discussed, the gendered metaphors of Rambo litigator and
mothering paralegal establish and maintain a hierarchical and complementary relationship between hegemonic masculinity and hegemonic femininity.
By virtue of their profession, women litigators contest this relationship and
therein embody oppositional femininities. Various degrees of opposition are
reflected in the gender strategies employed by these lawyers. Women who appropriated *resisting and reshaping the adversarial role* are not merely contesting the firm association between men and litigation but also the hegemonic
masculine emotional labor of *gamesmanship* and contributing to challenging
the naturalized and uncontested status of this toxic form of emotional labor.
Lawyers who adopted *splitting the roles versus distancing* only contested hegemonic masculine emotional labor outside the courtroom and thus contributed to its reaffirmation inside the courtroom and status as constituting
professional success. By not challenging the established status of hegemonic
masculine forms of emotional labor as a signifier of professional success, they
are complicit with hegemonic masculinity and contribute to its dominance
(Connell 1995, 79). While *talk like a lawyer, think like a lawyer, act like a lawyer* is clearly a strategy that challenges an assumption that women are unsuitable for litigation, the strategy contributes to reaffirming the superiority of
hegemonic masculine forms of emotional labor and inferiority of hegemonic
feminine emotional labor. Of these strategies, only *resisting and reshaping the
adversarial role* contributes to destabilizing the firm association between a
masculinized *gamesmanship* form of emotional labor and litigation and
equalizing gender relations.

Some discussion of the stereotypically feminine paralegal profession can
provide additional insights into the gendered emotional labor expected of male
and female professionals. Pierce (1995, 83) applies the gendered metaphor of
mothering paralegal to capture the often underappreciated supportive work
and feminized emotional labor that women paralegals are typically expected to
perform. The emotional labor requirements of paralegals involve deference
and caretaking (Pierce 1995, 85). Deferential emotional labor is accomplished

by not criticizing attorneys' written work or professional habits, which reinforces the construction of their professional identities (Pierce 1995, 89–95). Paralegals perform deferential emotional labor by unconditionally accepting lawyers' continual criticism of their work and challenges to their professional competence but never disputing their professional judgment or expertise.

Female paralegals are also expected to serve as quasi emotional caretakers of both attorneys and clients (Pierce 1995, 98–101). Emotional caretaking is accomplished by displaying a pleasant demeanor, providing reassurance, and serving as emotional arbiters of attorneys' feelings. Paralegals perform this invisible form of emotional labor by reassuring attorneys in an attempt to alleviate their work-related anxieties and concerns. This emotional labor also involves the crucial task of allying witness anxieties at critical times throughout the entire litigation process. In addition, paralegals serve as interpreters of attorneys' emotional outbursts or other social infractions by apologizing on their behalf and thereby repairing damaged relationships. These examples illustrate the feminized nature of the paralegal professional and gendered assumption that women are naturally suited for this type of work.

A major implication of the discussion of emotional labor in the legal profession is that it reflects both the gendered nature and gendered division of emotional labor. As Hochschild (1983) adeptly demonstrated, masculinized occupations such as bill collector and physician tend to sanction more authoritative forms of emotional labor, while feminized professions such as flight attendant and nurse tend to privilege deferential displays of emotional labor. Similarly, my analysis has shown how the requisite emotional labor for lawyers is gendered masculine while that expected of paralegals is gendered feminine. Not only is emotional labor fundamentally gendered, but men and women are also held accountable to perform certain types of emotional labor due to sex category membership.

The gendering of certain professions and accompanying forms of emotional labor is not inherently problematic because individuals possess agency to accomplish masculinity or femininity regardless of biological sex. This was exemplified by men and women police officers whose emotional restraint exemplified middle-class masculine values. However, the existence and application of a sexual double standard regarding expected performances of emotional labor is troubling because it contributes to the subordination of femininity. The application of a sexual double standard was strikingly evident in the case of male paralegals who were excused from performing deferential emotional labor and emotional caretaking and instead allowed to display affective neutrality (Pierce 1995, 147). A double standard also manifested in other forms such as male paralegals' presumed professional competence and access to informal socialization and thus networking opportunities with male attorneys (Pierce 1995, 157). The firm association between masculinity, which is typically attributed to men, and professional competence enabled these men to subvert professional norms without sanction. In stark contrast, women lawyers who rejected and attempted to reformulate gamesmanship were not automatically regarded as professionally competent because of a disassociation between femininity and professional competence. This could explain why some lawyers chose either to conform to the masculine norm or split roles and still perform masculinized emotional labor in the courtroom. Although a certain degree of authority and professional competence may accompany the display of masculinized emotional labor, this gendered strategy inevitably contributes to the normalization and superiority of masculinity and denigration and inferiority of femininity.

In the next section, we will also see that while many corporations are gendered masculine, workplace cultures align along a gendered continuum from more masculine to more feminine. Therefore, a dichotomized conceptualization of corporations is simplistic and fails to capture the wide range of workplace contexts. Nevertheless, a fundamental contention between leadership and masculinity ensures that women managers can still face a double bind. Paralleling other nontraditional professions, women design creative strategies to ameliorate this tension and claim professional authority.

Emotional Labor in Corporate Management

The masculinized nature of corporate environments is suggested by the prevalence and circulation of war metaphors (e.g., *business men are warriors*) which encapsulate the idealized values of aggression, courage, and competitiveness that constitute professional success (Koller 2004, 5–6). The business profession can be conceptualized as a type of strategic warfare that involves mobilizing the weaponry of technical expertise, verbal persuasion, and mental astuteness to outmaneuver and defeat one's opponents. As a result, norms of appropriate emotional labor include aggressiveness, competitiveness, and decisiveness (Holmes 2006, 6; Koller 2004, 6; Wajcman 1998, 49).

Management research makes a distinction between transactional and transformational leadership styles (Holmes 2006, 63). Managers who adopt a *transactional* style attempt to meet organizational objectives through the use of power, position, and institutionally based authority (Baxter 2008, 201; Holmes 2006, 63). In contrast, a *transformational* leadership style is built upon the core values of personal respect, openness, and social responsibility (Baxter 2008, 202; Holmes 2006, 63). The former style is typically associated with masculinity because it foregrounds authoritarian decision making and forming hierarchical relationships and latter with femininity as it privileges democratic decision making and formulating egalitarian relationships. Nevertheless, the most effective leaders do not restrict themselves to the use of one style, but dynamically combine elements of both styles as they negotiate the intersection between workplace and gendered norms (Baxter 2008, 216–17; Holmes 2006, 211).

Recent research emphasizes the highly situated and contextually dependent nature of the management styles or emotional labor which characterizes corporations (Baxter 2003; Fletcher 1999; Holmes 2006; Wajcman 1998). In light of these insights, it needs to be underscored that workplaces exist along a continuum from more feminized to more masculinized organizational cultures. Whereas some larger organizations may be characterized as masculine due to their hierarchal organization and competitive atmosphere, the workplace cultures of smaller, nonprofit organization may be classified as feminine because of a more egalitarian structure and collaborative environment.

One result of empirical research which focuses on the highly situated and contextually variant nature of organizational cultures is the emergence of a distinctively feminine form of emotional labor or *relational practice* (Fletcher 1999). Based on a study of female design engineers, Fletcher (1999, 2) defines relational practice as "the ability to work effectively with others, understanding the emotional contexts in which work gets done." Relational practice (hereafter RP) solidifies interpersonal relationships, which promotes the achievement of organizational objectives. Despite RP's compatibility with a transformational leadership style, it is often rendered inconsequential and thus *disappeared* due to its association with femininity (Fletcher 1999, 2, 91). Fletcher (1999, 48) distinguishes between four interrelated forms of RP which she labels *preserving, mutual empowering, self-achieving,* and *creating team.*

Preserving activities support the successful completion of a project (Fletcher 1999, 48)—for example, assisting colleagues with tasks that fall outside your own job description, but nevertheless support the timely and auspicious completion of a project (50). Notably, preserving activities challenge the notion that individual achievement and ability are the sine qua non of professional success and reframe professional accomplishment as a mutual endeavor which requires collaboration.

Mutual empowering is "behavior intended to enable others' achievement and contribution to the project" (Fletcher 1999, 55). Similar to how the paralegals whom Pierce (1995) studied often served as attorneys' emotional interpretators, mutual empowering involves activities such as apologizing or explaining on behalf of others to prevent the formation of bad feelings between colleagues which could negatively impact the organizational objective of project completion (Fletcher 1999, 59–60). Mutual empowering is also accomplished by providing colleagues with information that might assist them. As an example, Fletcher (1999, 63) cites an engineer who alerts her colleague to an issue with his work prior to a performance review meeting. Neither assisting others nor accepting that assistance is viewed as a sign of codependence or weakness, but is definitive of the type of democratic relationships normative in workplaces which value RP. Crucially, mutual empowering repositions a view of power as an individual possession to that of a shared resource which is distributed among colleagues.

Self-achieving involves "using relational skills to enhance one's professional growth and effectiveness" (Fletcher 1999, 65). For example, one engineer discussed how the favors or assistance she provided to her colleagues are usually reciprocated (Fletcher 1999, 67). Unlike mutual empowering, which is oriented toward enabling others, self-achievement is relational work that is performed for personal advancement. Despite the association between self-achieving and personal goals, meeting those goals is accomplished through eliciting the mutual cooperation of team members. Hence, similar to other forms of RP, teamwork is an essential and definitive component of self-achieving.

Creating team indexes "activities intended to foster group life" (Fletcher 1999, 73). Creating team is behavior oriented toward strengthening relationships between individuals that contributes to the formation of a more convivial workplace culture. Small talk is a prime example of relational activity that establishes and strengthens bonds between colleagues (Holmes 2006, 86). Creating team also surfaces as the facilitation of interactions between individuals who do not usually interact or reduce tense interpersonal relationships and in the process foster collaboration and interdependence (Fletcher 1999, 77).

The gendered emotional labor of relational practice also has implications for the relationship between masculinity and femininity. The more feminized relational practice and more masculine forms of emotional labor form a complementary but not necessarily hierarchical relationship, so these forms of emotional labor can be combined and receive equal validation. The complementary relationship becomes clearer when we compare relational practice with more masculine emotional labor. For instance, preserving corresponds to self-advancement, mutual empowering to competition, and creating team to individualism. Nonetheless, if relational practice and more masculine forms of emotional labor exist in a hierarchical relationship, then masculine forms of emotional labor and ultimately masculinity prevail as superior to femininity. Relational practice has transformative potential as it is built on a principle of destabilizing rigid hierarchies and power relationships, so workplace contexts which are committed to this form of emotional labor may contribute to equalizing gender relations. Of course, the normalization of more feminine forms of emotional labor alone will not equalize gender relations in the workplace. Crucial steps must also be taken to eradicate discriminatory employment practices, reduce working mothers' domestic burden, and de-gender masculinist workplace environments.

Fletcher's study demonstrates how relational practice, a feminized form of emotional labor, is vital to promote collaboration and teamwork, thereby fostering collegiality which is conducive to meeting organizational objectives. Crucially, however, Fletcher (1999, 2, 91) argues that because RP is culturally coded feminine behavior it is not only devalued but also deliberately disappeared from the organizational screen. Fletcher's findings endorse the overall argument of this book that femininity is culturally denigrated and, in the case of RP, rendered subordinate to a masculine logic of effectiveness which sanctions self-promotion, autonomy, and competition (Fletcher 1999, 90).

In spite of Fletcher's (1999, 3, 91) assertion that RP is quintessentially feminine emotional labor and is subsequently undervalued, the organizational context significantly impacts both the status and gendering of RP. Fletcher's claim about the denigrated status of RP is arguably true in the masculine workplace culture that she studied; however, RP is positively valued in more feminized workplace contexts and consequently definitive of professional success in some workplaces such as those committed to mobilizing transformational management principles. In addition, RP has multiple manifestations which vary according to organizational context and hence should not be regarded as exclusively feminine behavior (Holmes 2006, 93, 104).

Holmes (2006) provides an expanded conceptualization of RP based upon her empirical research which was conducted in a wide array of workplace contexts from large bureaucratic organizations to small workplaces and factories. Holmes found that RP is not only highly valued in some contexts but also has both feminine and masculine manifestations (Holmes 2006, 93, 104). In fact, some women managers use RP along with humor and narrative to resolve the double bind stemming from the incompatibility of their professional and gendered identities (Holmes 2006, 211).

Humor is a powerful discursive resource that women managers can draw on as they attempt to resolve the ubiquitous double bind (Holmes 2006, 109, 118). Humor emerges in a range of forms from more self-aggrandizing and contestive masculine style of humor to more self-deprecating and collaborative feminine humor (Holmes 2006, 109). For instance, Sam, a board member, implicitly criticized the length of Jill's meetings with the comment, "Keep going until there's only one person standing." Undiscouraged, Jill laughs and wittily responds, "Oh, you've been to our board meetings before" (Holmes 2006, 120). Jill's response can be interpreted as integrating aspects of both masculine and feminine forms of humor. Jill's reply supports Sam's claim that the meetings are indeed long, but it is constructed in a contestive manner. As a result, Jill's comment is sardonic and thus masculine in style but supportive and therefore feminine in terms of content.

Jill can also be seen as performing relational practice through her use of humor. Some leaders who possess a more hierarchical view of workplace relations might interpret Sam's comment as an instantiation of insubordination and respond with anger or a defense of meeting protocol. In contrast, Jill's response mitigates hierarchical relationships by using humor to build solidarity and thus create team with her employees. Jill's use of humor to present herself as an authoritative leader who is also receptive to employee feedback nicely demonstrates how relational practice can consist of both masculine and feminine components.

Workplace narratives are another discursive strategy women can use to resolve the dilemma of enacting a professional identity while remaining accountably feminine (Holmes 2006, 174). Narratives provide a channel for leaders to emphasize their competence through constructing heroic masculinized stories or attenuate that authority by telling self-deprecating feminine anecdotes (Holmes 2006, 176–205). For example, Leila, a senior manager in a government organization, constructed a narrative which presented her as a problem solver and thus competent manager but was also self-deprecating (Holmes 2006, 186–87). Leila recounted how she attempted to read the phone number off a flyer on a van while she was driving. Humorously, Leila depicted how after several failed attempts, she finally got close enough to the van so that she could read the phone number. The significance of this narrative is that the service advertised on the flyer offered a potential solution to an ongoing problem the team faced, so Leila presented herself as a problem solver through this narrative.

Consideration of the workplace context and accompanying norms is once again indispensable to obtain a comprehensive interpretation of this narrative. In this more feminine workplace context, Leila's subordinates might label her as overconfident for explicitly asserting her competence and thereby overstepping the boundaries of dominant femininity. Hence, Leila can be seen as constructing a narrative which simultaneously demonstrated her problem-solving ability and humanized or perhaps feminized her by presenting her as imperfect and prone to mistakes.

Unlike men, whose professional and gender identities align, women have to expend extra discursive work to manage the incongruence between their gender and professional identities (Holmes 2006, 183). Although self-deprecating in style, Leila's narrative is primarily a success story which again demonstrates how women can combine elements of femininity and masculinity as they attempt to manage the potential conflict between an authoritative professional identity on the one hand and gendered accountability on the other (Holmes 2006, 184, 190). At the same time, and somewhat paradoxically, women who adopt a self-deprecating style also risk being perceived as professionally incompetent because their leadership style misaligns with workplace norms (Holmes 2006, 190; Kendall 2004, 75). Despite their best efforts, professional women are sometimes unable to resolve the double bind and successfully construct a professional identity while remaining accountably femininie.

Narrative can also be viewed as a form of relational practice. For instance, Leila's narrative can be seen as exemplifying preserving, creating team, and self-achieving. The narrative served the indispensable function of demonstrating to her subordinates the importance of constantly searching for potential solutions to work-related problems. In addition, Leila built solidarity and created team with her subordinates by constructing a comical persona, which somewhat ameliorated their status differences. Although self-deprecating in form, the narrative also served the instrumental and thus self-achieving function of resolving the double bind. Much like humor, narrative is a flexible discursive resource which performs multiple functions.

Holmes's participants utilized humor and narrative to resolve the double bind posed by the incompatibility of their sex category membership and professional identity and simultaneously construct oppositional femininities. At the same time, it needs to be underscored that narrative and humor are forms of relational practice which contribute to breaking down rigid hierarchies and occupational boundaries. Although Jill and Leila appropriated masculine forms of humor and narrative, these communicative social actions ultimately served the purpose of preserving, creating team, and self-achieving. Therefore, we can view Leila and Jill as resisting hegemonic masculine values of personal advancement and competitive individualism and appropriating feminine forms of emotional labor to successfully perform their professional identities and equalize gender relations. In this case, masculine and feminine forms of emotional labor form a complementary but not hierarchical relationship and serve the emancipatory potential of equalizing gender relations.

The next section focuses on the priesthood which has been an exclusively male profession until relatively recently. Similar to previously discussed professions, women priests face a double bind between enacting their professional identities and remaining accountable to hegemonic femininity. Consequently, women priests mobilize different strategies to resolve this bind.

Emotional Labor in the Priesthood

Following a long and acrimonious battle, the first women priests were ordained in the Church of England in 1994. Similar to police work, law, and corporate management, women have faced resistance for attempting to enter a stereotypically masculine profession. However, the priesthood is fundamentally different from the previously discussed occupations in that it can be viewed as an instantiation of socially and institutionally sanctioned male gender-crossing (Walsh 2001, 192). Although the priesthood has traditionally been an all-male enclave, the job requires the deployment of traditionally feminine characteristics such as empathy, compassion, and nurturance. Therefore, male priests accomplish their professional identities and thus achieve power and status through performing feminine values in the public sphere (Walsh 2001, 192). Priests aspiring to hold pastorships must also exhibit more masculine characteristics such as leadership ability. A significant contrast from women priests is that male priests do not face a double bind between performing their professional identities and masculine accountability because the association between the priesthood and femininity remains unacknowledged. Much like RP, the connection between femininity and the priesthood is frequently missing, which again illustrates how hegemonic femininity occupies a subordinate position vis-à-vis hegemonic masculinity.

Despite the inroads women have made into this profession, women priests are still accountably feminine. For instance, women are held accountable to norms which emphasize service, self-giving, self-effacement, and other-empowerment (Walsh 2001, 166). These values become the basis for assigning them more pastoral work which purportedly taps their latent abilities, but does not result in the high visibility and the necessary recognition for promotion (Bagilhole 2002, 165). In order to receive promotions, priests must demonstrate their leadership ability through more visible work such as chairing parish meetings, preaching at services, and heading parishes. In line with my discussion of other nontraditional professions, women priests face a double bind between claiming authority and professional status while remaining accountable to hegemonic femininity.

The gender accountability of men and women priests reflects the hierarchical and complementary relationship definitive of hegemonic masculinity and hegemonic femininity. Based on an ideology of corporeal difference, women priests are held accountable to altruism and empathy while men priests are accountable to professional competence and leadership ability. These gender characteristics are utilized to affirm an unequal relationship between men and women, masculinity and femininity. As a result, women are channeled into less visible and arguably less valued caregiving work while men are channeled into pastoral positions which result in opportunities for further advancement. In spite or perhaps because of their feminine accountability, women priests deployed a number of strategies to resolve or at least ameliorate the tension between their feminine and professional identities.

One strategy that women priests employed was to downplay their femininity and emphasize their professional role (Walsh 2001, 189). These women emphasized how gender was unconnected to their professional role and some even problematized the nomenclature *woman priest*. In order to disassociate from femininity and accomplish their professional identity, some women chose to wear dark-colored clothing and no jewelry (Walsh 2001, 190). Presumably, these women were able to command a certain degree of authority by adopting a masculine demeanor; however, they also contributed to the overall cultural denigration of femininity by severing any connection with femininity.

Other women claimed a professional identity by oscillating between emphasizing aspects of their femininity in certain situations and deemphasizing it in others (Walsh 2001, 193). For instance, feminine qualities such as empathy and sensitivity could be seen as assets during emotionally charged situations such as funerals. However, these qualities would not increase their professional status during mixed-sex meetings, so they chose to suppress them during these times. This strategy exemplifies the necessity of contextually sensitive gendered performances in conjunction with the norms which constitute certain situations. As previously discussed, workplace norms can override gender and strongly influence the accomplishment of professional identities.

Another strategy is to unapologetically perform femininity and emphasize the unique skills and qualities women bring to the ministry (Walsh 2001, 195). These women were careful to emphasize that feminine qualities are not natural or inevitable, but deliberately employed as alternatives to masculine norms. For example, one priest contrasted her more egalitarian leadership style with the more authoritarian style typically appropriated by men (Walsh 2001, 195). Problematically, others may construe this strategy as an instantiation of corporeal differences predisposing women and men to perform different social roles and contribute to a gender division of labor within the priesthood. Women's *innate* pastoral skills can become the basis for assigning them to subordinate organizational roles while men occupy more prestigious positions (Walsh 2001, 197, 207). On the other hand, the strategy can provide increased visibility to feminine qualities which enhance one's job performance and arguably should be appropriated by both men and women priests.

The professional strategies utilized by women priests contest women's subordinate position in relation to their male counterparts and thus indicate they are accomplishing oppositional femininities. The first strategy involves appropriating masculinity and distancing oneself from femininity. In this case, women are opposing elements of dominant femininity but concomitantly legitimizing an asymmetrical relationship between masculine and feminine forms of emotional labor and accommodating gender hegemony. Women who utilized the second strategy shifted between performing masculine and feminine forms of emotional labor. These women opposed neither masculinity nor femininity per se but instead a rigid dichotomization between gendered forms of emotional labor, and in the process potentially contributed to de-gendering and democratizing gender relations. At first glance, the women who adopted the final strategy, unapologetically performing femininity, do not appear to be opposing but instead appropriating femininity. Although this is true, they are opposing the unequal relationship between masculinity and femininity, which posits women and femininity as unsuitable for leadership positions within the church. Hence, these women can be seen as contributing to equalizing the relationship between feminine and masculine professional styles and democratizing gender relations.

Women priests face a unique situation compared to the previously discussed professions. I discussed how police officers, lawyers, and corporate executives confront quintessentially masculine workplace cultures which are dominated by men and resistant toward women. The priesthood was exclusively male until recently; however, the workplace culture and expected emotional labor are arguably feminine. Many of priests' duties such as visiting the sick, comforting the bereaved, and counseling parishioners require feminine forms of emotional labor such as empathy, compassion, and nurturance. As a result, women priests find themselves in a paradoxical situation where their gender and supposed innate caregiving capacity predisposes them to the profession but ironically contributes to their marginalization within the profession. Significantly, women are relegated to certain backstage pastoral positions which do not result in the same degree of professional prestige and financial remuneration as parish pastoralships and other leadership positions. Again, we see how a gendered division of labor is reproduced in the public sphere, and women are confined to backstage, supportive roles while men assume center stage.

Gender Relations in Workplace Institutions

In this section I discuss the implications of the performance of gender within nontraditional occupations for each of the four dimensions of gender relations. Although I separately discuss each dimension of gender relations, it needs to be underscored that they do not operate in isolation but intersect with and thus dynamically influence the other dimensions.

Power Relations

Inegalitarian power relations were reflected not only by men's overrepresentation in police work, litigation, corporate management, and the priesthood but also by their monopolization of prestigious specializations within these professions. I discussed how men wield power through employment in prestigious professional specializations such as litigation and monopolize corporate and clergical administrative positions. Even token male paralegals are treated more professionally than their female counterparts and thus awarded a certain degree of power exclusively based upon their sex category membership. Consequently, women who work in nontraditional professions not only threaten men's hold on economic and social power but also their masculinity.

Production Relations

Production relations were reflected by an unequal gendered division of domestic labor where women either solely managed the household or juggled their career responsibilities with the second shift of housework and childcare responsibilities. Men, by contrast, are released from an expectation that they participate in domestic life due to the hegemony of the male career ideology which posits their career responsibilities as primary. Unlike professional women, marriage and fatherhood do not hinder, but in fact enhance, men's job performance and thus access to promotional opportunities (Wajcman 1998, 81). The domestic support provided by a wife or paid caregiver ensures that men can completely commit themselves to their careers and thus are better situated for promotional opportunities (Wajcman 1998, 38–39).

Production relations are also reflected in family-friendly policies which exclusively focus on helping women combine paid and unpaid labor and therefore are not gender neutral but presuppose that women manage the household (Bagilhole 2002, 79–80). The expectation that men work outside and women inside the home is also reflected in an ideal worker's career path which is defined by long hours, uninterrupted length of service, and geographic mobility. As this career trajectory presupposes continuous employment, working mothers' career advancement prospects are reduced by taking maternity leave. A serious effort to support working parents would involve the creation of family-friendly policies which create more flexible employment options and cultivate workplace cultures which facilitate the combination of work and parenting responsibilities.

Emotional Relations

Emotional relations were reflected by the gendering and gendered division of emotional labor. Emotional labor is gendered more masculine or feminine in conjunction with the workplace norms. Therefore, an economy of affect was normative in police work, gamesmanship was commonplace in litigation, and both feminine and masculine forms of emotional labor were the norm in corporations and the priesthood. Significantly, feminized forms of emotional labor such as relational practice often support workplace objectives but are dismissed as peripheral to the primary concerns of workplace business. This illustrates how despite the crucial function that feminine forms of emotional labor play, it is disappeared to reify the connection between masculinity and public work and marginalize femininity.

Janet Holmes's (2006) work provided a more complex and nuanced picture of the highly situated and contextually dependent nature of emotional labor. Holmes claims that the validation of specific forms of emotional labor depends upon workplace norms and that emotional labor itself can combine both feminine and masculine elements. As a result, feminine forms of emotional labor are sometimes superior to masculine forms; nonetheless, the entrenched association between participation in the paid labor market and masculinity can make it difficult for women to construct their professional and gendered identities.

Symbolic Relations

Symbolic relations are reflected in gender differences discourses which position men and women as essentially different and thus suited to perform different, albeit unequally valued, social tasks. As a result, public work and professional success are often conflated with masculinity and private work and caregiving with femininity. Problematically, women's reproductive capacity can be used as a rationalization against hiring them in top-level positions and instead relegating them to the lower-ranking *mommy track* because their domestic responsibilities will purportedly infringe upon their ability to perform professional responsibilities (Lorber 1994, 235, 285).

Socially constructed notions of femininity and their supposed incompatibility with paid labor contribute to the formation of a well-documented and pervasive double bind for professional women. Women face a catch-22 situation where if they appropriate masculine styles of leadership or forms of emotional labor they subvert femininity. On the other hand, if they enact feminine leadership norms or displays of emotional labor, they are rendered ineffective leaders. Relational practice, humor, and narrative are discursive resources that professional women can use as they attempt to resolve the tension between their gender and professional identities.

Oppositional Femininities' Role in Troubling Gender Relations

Women working in nontraditional occupations can be seen as oppositional femininities because the performance of their professional identities necessitates that they sometimes practice masculine forms of emotional labor, thereby threatening men's undisputed monopolization of this resource and ultimately the superiority of hegemonic masculinity. As a result, women sometimes oppose masculine forms of emotional labor, feminine forms of emotional labor, or the fundamental asymmetry between masculine and feminine forms of emotional labor where masculinity is superior to femininity. Indeed, *oppositional femininities* encompass a broad range of gender strategies, including token women who conform to masculine values and thereby explicitly challenge the principle that these values are men's exclusive possession. It also includes women who employ more diverse strategies which accommodate, resist, and combine feminine and masculine forms of emotional labor. Therefore, oppositional femininities cover a wide range of femininities which explicitly and implicitly challenge hegemonic masculinity. Due to the diverse range of oppositional femininities, we need to distinguish between oppositional femininities whose power stems from practicing hegemonic masculinity and those who challenge the unequal relationship between hegemonic masculinity and hegemonic femininity and thus contribute to potentially equalizing gender relations.

As paid employment is the sine qua non of hegemonic masculinity, women employed in nontraditional professions accrue a degree of social power through their professional statuses. Power materializes in the form of the high salaries and social prestige accompanying these professions. Professional women challenge the assumption that these nontraditional occupations are exclusively male terrain and thus contribute to a more equal distribution of material wealth and social power between men and women.

Women working in nontraditional occupations challenge production relations through participation in the paid labor market. Although they challenge the assumption that the paid labor market is unquestionably men's territory, a new division of labor is emerging where women assume the double burden of both domestic and professional responsibilities. Hence, women's participation in the paid labor market alone does not signify the emergence of more egalitarian gender relations when it is unaccompanied by an equal redistribution of domestic responsibilities among couples. For this reason, women who unquestionably assume the second shift reify the hegemony of the male career ideology and contribute to the ascendance of hegemonic masculinity.

Women employed in nontraditional occupations contest emotional relations by demonstrating that women can display the appropriate emotional labor required by these professions. However, we also saw how women had to employ different strategies to resolve the double bind and thus could not unequivocally display the requisite emotional labor due to a tension between leadership and femininity. Nevertheless, women's unique appropriation of various forms of emotional labor may provide feminine forms of emotional labor with increased visibility and contribute to increasing their value. I endorse Holmes's (2006, 67) view that women's appropriation of masculine discursive styles (and vice versa) may result in de-gendering and re-categorizing them as neutral leadership tools.

Women working in nontraditional occupations challenge the symbolic construction of men as naturally suited for these professions and demonstrate that women can adapt to a range of workplace cultures. Gender differences can no longer be used as a rationalization to exclude women from paid employment. Notably, these women did not simply conform to masculine norms but performed leadership through diverse strategies. For these reasons, women employed in nontraditional occupations are not simply conforming to masculine norms but doing gender and leadership differently and contributing to undermining the superiority of masculine forms of emotional labor and leadership style as the archetype of professional success. As men accomplish hegemonic masculinity through constructing a hierarchical relationship with hegemonic femininity, it is unsurprising that men create obstacles to hinder women's movement into well-paid, high-prestige professions.

One explanation for men's resistance toward and marginalization of women entering nontraditional occupations is the threat they pose. Women not only threaten men's exclusive hold on material wealth and social power, but also, and significantly, they threaten hegemonic masculinity. Women who demonstrate professional competence trouble the heterosexual matrix, which posits masculinity and femininity as polarized opposites, through de-gendering leadership and blurring the masculinity/femininity hierarchical distinction. Regarding some men's resistance to women cadets, Kimmel (2000, 503) points out the following:

> Thus, while VMI and the Citadel appear on the surface to be about men's natural superiority over women, they are, underneath, about precisely its opposite—the fragility of that hierarchy, the vulnerability to pollution and dilution, and the terror of emasculation that would be attendance on equality of opportunity.

One reading of men's resistance to women entering nontraditional occupations is that they threaten an ideology of men's natural superiority over women (Connell 1995, 83). Oppositional femininities trouble the unequal relationship definitive of hegemonic masculinity and hegemonic femininity and promulgate the transformation of a patriarchal gender order.

Crisis Tendencies

Women working in nontraditional professions, who exemplify oppositional femininities, can contribute to the formation of crisis tendencies which promote both respect for greater gender diversity and the formation of more egalitarian gender relations. Crucially, these women did not perform their professional identities through the mere appropriation of masculinity and therein serve as handmaidens to its ascendance. Instead, they uniquely combined elements of masculinity and femininity and collectively challenged the masculine gendering of leadership. Conceivably, the movement of women into nontraditional occupations accompanied by the normalization of masculine and feminine leadership styles will dismantle the connection between masculinity and leadership and result in increased tolerance for diverse leadership styles.

Discussion

Similar to chapter 3, my discussion of the workplace has illuminated how the embodiment of hegemonic femininity disempowers women and therefore can be seen as a paradoxical privilege. In the public domain of work, hegemonic femininity occupies a subordinate position vis-à-vis hegemonic masculinity and accordingly supports its ascendance. This is reflected in women's underappreciated domestic role and the disappearing of feminine forms of emotional labor. However, I also demonstrated how feminine forms of emotional labor perform a crucial function in certain workplace contexts, particularly those committed to the principles of transformational leadership.

The paradoxical nature of embodying hegemonic femininity is reflected by the different evaluation of women and men when they exhibit feminine characteristics. If workplace organizations are truly committed to implementing transformational management styles, then feminine and masculine characteristics collectively will constitute effective leadership and the concept will become de-gendered. However, Holmes (2006, 216) makes the important point that it would be ironic if men are rewarded for extending their discursive styles while women are labeled ineffective leaders for exhibiting feminine leadership styles, which have paradoxically been undervalued in the past due to their association with femininity. Holmes's point demonstrates how the value of feminine characteristics can increase when men appropriate them and they become associated with masculinity. Notably, any connection with femininity is unacknowledged and instead renamed transformational leadership. Although Holmes's careful analysis has demonstrated the gamut of styles that effective leaders employ, the fact that women face a double bind indicates that feminine and masculine strategies are evaluated differently when mobilized by men and women. Paradoxically, feminine characteristics are becoming de-gendered and included in the repertoire of characteristics which constitute transformational leadership when mobilized by men, but are denigrated when employed by women. I contend that this is a strategy that men utilize to disempower women and ensure that any connection between effective leadership and femininity is rendered obsolete. Although leadership is gradually becoming de-gendered, sex category membership can still be strategically invoked to disempower women and ensure the ascendance of hegemonic masculinity.

Conclusion

The first part of this chapter discussed how the hierarchical relationship between hegemonic masculinity and hegemonic femininity is reflected in gender divisions of labor. Masculine labor receives a paid wage, social prestige, and public recognition while feminine labor is unpaid, undervalued, and largely unrecognized. As a result, hegemonic masculinity is associated with individual accomplishments and professional success which are superior to hegemonic feminine practices such as other-empowerment and pastoral work. The cultural exaltation of masculinity is also reflected in the gender division of labor where married men completely devote themselves to their careers while married women are saddled with the second shift of domestic work.

The gendered division of labor is not only confined to a distinction between paid and unpaid labor but also occurs within occupations and specializations. Reflecting the cultural idealization of masculinity and denigration of femininity, masculine professions and specializations such as corporate management and litigation result in higher salaries and are awarded a higher level of prestige than feminine ones such as paralegal work and family law. Hence, women's access to professions which result in high salaries and institutional power are severely limited.

The second part of the chapter focused on the double bind facing professional women due to a fundamental incompatibility between their gender and professional identities. Although workplaces exist along a gendered continuum, leadership is apparently gendered masculine, so the mere presence of women leaders challenges this gendered norm and ultimately threatens male power. Therefore, men can undermine women's authority by holding them accountable to femininity.

I discussed how the double bind is particularly salient concerning the display and gendering of emotional labor. As women are accountable to femininity, they are expected to display feminine forms of emotional labor; however, masculine emotional labor is normative in certain workplace contexts. Therefore, women can face a dilemma between their feminine accountability and displaying masculinized emotional labor. In order to resolve this bind, women draw on discursive devices such as relational practice, narrative, and humor, and devise a whole range of strategies from appropriating to eschewing elements of masculine and feminine emotional labor. Notably, the effectiveness of specific discursive devices and strategies intersects with and thus is contingent upon workplace norms.

The final section of the chapter argued that women working in nontraditional occupations contribute to challenging the naturalization of a masculine leadership style and equalizing gender relations. Significantly, these women did not simply conform to and thus reify masculine workplace norms, but uniquely integrated elements of masculine and feminine discursive styles and thereby contributed to de-gendering leadership. Similar to chapter 3, oppositional femininities contest elements of masculinity, femininity, and sometimes the unequal relationship between hegemonic masculinity and hegemonic femininity, and accordingly can be seen as agents of social change.

The next chapter shifts focus from an analysis of how individuals accomplish femininities within key social institutions to an analysis of media representations of femininity. Due to its pervasiveness, the media is another salient venue to investigate constructions of hegemonic and oppositional femininities.

5

Media Representations of Femininities

This chapter represents a slight departure from the preceding analytical chapters. While school and the workplace are key sites where individuals actively construct their gender identities against the backdrop of social structure, the media is fundamentally different because it disseminates gendered images and thus fictitious representations of masculinities and femininities. Nevertheless, we cannot ignore the media's power to not merely represent but also construct notions of dominant, hegemonic, subordinate, and oppositional femininities and masculinities at the regional level (Litosseliti 2006, 92). At the same time, viewers are not merely passive recipients of these images, but possess agency to critically examine and contest the legitimacy of such representations. Whereas some women and girls may idolize and attempt to emulate these images, others will reject and resist these representations. In either case, media images serve as cultural templates for idealized notions of masculinity and femininity which actual men and women can be held accountable to. As a result, media programs should not be dismissed as innocuous entertainment but viewed as disseminators of culturally idealized gendered images which merit critical scrutiny and analysis.

This chapter concerns the construction of dominant, hegemonic, subordinate, and oppositional femininities within fictional media. I have selected several relatively recent popular films and a television series which capture diverse representations of femininities. The first section of the chapter focuses on blockbuster Disney films produced during the late 1980s through the 1990s which overwhelmingly present very traditional representations of femininity.

In the second part of the chapter I focus on *Fatal Attraction, Bridget Jones's Diary*, and *Sex and the City*, which portray single women during the 1980s, 1990s, and 2000s and disseminate more ambiguous images of femininity. These media present diverse images of single life which simultaneously invoke and subvert stereotypical images of unmarried women. Despite their subversive potential, the dominant heteronormative narrative dispersed by these narratives is one of women who are fulfilled through long-term heterosexual romance.

Significantly, these media disseminate complex representations of femininity which confirm, contest, and potentially reformulate dominant femininities. Even within the same film, progressive and retrogressive representations of femininity can coexist, thus illustrating the insidious nature of gendered media representations. For this reason, the media is an appropriate site to investigate the representation, production, and reproduction of various masculinities and femininities.

Disney Introduction

Due to the widespread popularity of Disney theme parks, films, and merchandise, Giroux (1996, 92) maintains that Disney has achieved the status of a cultural icon. The iconic status ascribed to Disney and Disney film subsequently provides these celluloid representations a degree of cultural legitimacy and authority to not simply represent but also construct gender. Young children are exposed to a seemingly innocuous form of entertainment which in reality disseminates strikingly conventional representations of masculinity and femininity. Lamb and Brown (2006, 59) point out how young children under age six cannot distinguish television shows from commercials; similarly, children are unable to critically scrutinize the gendered images produced by Disney which arguably impact their notions of gender. As a result, Disney films cannot simply be dismissed as harmless entertainment but merit critical scrutiny and analysis.

I next focus attention on analyzing pervasive gendered representations that circulate in *The Little Mermaid* (1989), *Beauty and the Beast* (1991), *Pocahontas* (1995), and *Mulan* (1998). In the span of roughly a decade, Disney produced a string of hugely popular blockbusters. The success of these films extended well beyond the box office to encompass revenue generated from sales of merchandise, film soundtracks, videotapes, and DVDs. The success of these films may be attributable to many people's familiarity with these fairy tales and thus their place in North American (and other societies') cultural consciousness, although their origins lie elsewhere. These films are retellings of traditional fairytales, which at first glance appear to portray strong female characters and thus nonstereotypical gendered representations. However, a more careful reading reveals that Disney merely subverts aspects of dominant femininity only to feminize and thus subordinate female characters in other ways. A pervasive theme is that female characters are overwhelmingly portrayed as focused on and fulfilled by long-term heterosexual relationships, which Sunderland (2004, 60) refers to as an *incomplete woman* discourse. In stark contrast, male characters are represented as self-ambitious and goal driven, and romantic relationships are only a secondary concern. Consequently, the unequal relationship between hegemonic femininity and masculinity is reconstituted, not subverted. Dominant femininity is recreated from a passive maiden who waits for Prince Charming to a stronger character who actively pursues her prince. We see then the subtle workings of retrogressive gendered representations through the depiction of female characters who are not passive and ambitionless but whose ultimate goal is to capture Mr. Right.

The Little Mermaid

The Little Mermaid tells the story of the mermaid Ariel who is dissatisfied with life in the sea and utterly captivated by the human world. Nevertheless, Ariel's father, King Triton, is clear that contact between merpeople and humans is strictly forbidden. One evening, Ariel travels to the surface of the sea and coincidentally observes Prince Eric's birthday celebration onboard a ship. A storm interrupts the festivities and causes Eric's companions to escape in a lifeboat, while Eric attempts to rescue his dog and almost drowns in the process. Ariel prevents Eric's drowning and drags him ashore. Once Eric starts to wake up, Ariel quickly retreats to the ocean, but she is clearly in love with him. Notably, Ariel's fascination with the human world becomes reconstituted as enchantment with Eric.

King Triton is furious to learn that Ariel saved a human being and he disavows her desire to live in the human world which causes Ariel to seek the assistance of the sea witch Ursula. Ursula offers Ariel an enticing pact which could potentially enable her to live in the human world. The agreement states that Ariel will be transformed into a human being for three days during which time Eric must bestow the kiss of true love on her for her human state to remain permanent. If Eric fails to kiss her within the allocated time, Ariel will transform back into a mermaid and become Ursula's prisoner. In order to secure the deal, Ariel must offer her voice as payment to Ursula, and thus Ariel faces an additional challenge of capturing Eric's heart while speechless. Ursula assures Ariel that her appearance and the use of body language are sufficient to win Eric's affection and asserts that human men are not fond of talkative women. Ariel accepts the offer and is transformed into a human.

After Eric finds Ariel washed ashore on a beach, he brings her back to his palace. As they spend more time together, their relationship gradually becomes closer and Ursula is infuriated. In order to prevent their relationship from further developing, Ursula disguises herself as a beautiful young woman, Vanessa, who has Ariel's voice. She casts a spell on Eric who then falls in love with her and proclaims that they wish to be married, which understandably devastates Ariel.

Although Eric and Vanessa never actually marry, Ursula is able to buy enough time so that Ariel cannot fulfill the conditions of the contract and she becomes Ursula's prisoner. King Triton subsequently confronts Ursula and unsuccessfully attempts to destroy the contract with his trident. Ursula offers to trade Ariel's freedom for King Triton which he unhesitatingly accepts. Intoxicated by her newly acquired power, Ursula transfigures into a giant and is just about to kill Ariel when Eric mortally wounds Ursula and saves Ariel. Ursula's death results in all of her former prisoners transforming back into merpeople and King Triton is also restored to power.

The movie's ending follows a traditional fairy-tale narrative where the protagonists live happily ever after. King Triton realizes that Eric and Ariel are in love and transforms Ariel back into a human. The final scene shows their wedding which reasserts the importance of heterosexual romance for women.

Gender in The Little Mermaid

Many of Ariel's embodied gender actions make her an archetype of dominant femininity. However, as I indicated, Disney characters are not always straightforwardly classifiable as dominant or oppositional femininities, but instead create hybrid femininities which integrate subversive and traditionally feminine qualities. The power of dominant gendered images lies with their ability to construct hybrid femininities which superficially appear to contest but in fact reify the unequal relationship between hegemonic masculinity and hegemonic femininity.

Physical Appearance   Ariel's physical beauty and anorexic thinness make her an exemplar of dominant femininity. Since Ariel loses the capacity to speak, her appearance and to a certain extent charm are the main feminine resources she has to drawn on as she attempts to capture Eric's heart. Notably, Ursula reaffirms the importance of women's physical appearance when she states that Ariel's appearance and body language are sufficient to capture Eric's heart, and she also maintains that human men dislike overly talkative women. Ursula's comment invokes a popular stereotype of gossiping, talkative women who are apparently undesirable as partners for men. In addition to overemphasizing the importance of heterosexual love for women, this film foregrounds appearance as the sole feature women use to attract men's attention.

Sexuality The fact that children are the targeted consumers of these films requires that the characters' sexuality is toned down. Nevertheless, this film represents female sexuality as a virgin/whore dichotomy. Ariel embodies the morally pure, presumably virgin Madonna figure while Vanessa is a conniving seductress who is also a witch. Prior to Vanessa's arrival, Eric and Ariel appeared to be falling in love and heading toward a long-term commitment. Therefore, Eric's enchantment with Vanessa fictitiously portrays a female temptress who uses deception and sexual appeal to entice a man into infidelity and lure him away from his wife.

Self-Confidence Ariel possesses a degree of self-confidence which appears to subvert dominant femininity. For the majority of the movie, there are few indications that Ariel is unconfident about her ability to attract Eric. Accordingly, I would argue that since Ariel's confidence is not in relation to personal abilities but in her capacity to capture Eric's heart, Ariel does not subvert this component of dominant femininity. Rather, Ariel's primary goal of forming a nonplatonic relationship with Eric again reifies the principle that romantic relationships are of primary importance to women and mirrors earlier films such as *Snow White and the Seven Dwarfs* (1937), *Cinderella* (1950), and *Sleeping Beauty* (1959).

Eric and Ariel not only complement one another but also form a hierarchical relationship whereby Eric embodies hegemonic masculinity and Ariel embodies hegemonic femininity. They both embody many of the gendered, complementary characteristics constituting dominant forms of masculinity and femininity. Ariel is beautiful and petite while Eric is handsome and strong. Both characters are self-confident; however, Ariel's self-confidence is directed at capturing Eric's heart, while Eric's self-confidence focuses on rescuing Ariel from Ursula. Regarding sexuality, Eric appears to value heterosexual monogamy as he expressed a desire to find the woman who rescued him. However, and problematically, his infatuation with the girl who saved him is solely based upon conventional markers of dominant femininity—her beauty and voice—which say nothing about her personality. As Ariel cannot speak, Eric fails to recognize her as his rescuer. Concerning Ariel's sexuality, she is initially physically attracted to Eric; however, her entire existence is defined by capturing Eric's heart and thus appealing to his heterosexual desires. Therefore, there is an absent discourse of female desire (Tolman 2002, 14).

Although Eric embodies hegemonic masculinity and thus establishes a dominant position in relation to Ariel, this is not accomplished as a domineering patriarch but more subtly through the role of *hegemonic masculine heroic rescuer* (Messerschmidt 2010). In popular film, the masculine hero is represented as defeating an evil villain, saving a vulnerable female victim, and in the process constructing masculinity (Messerschmidt 2010, 58). Reflecting a slightly modified version of the hero narrative, Eric rescues Ariel from Ursula and concomitantly saves the merworld from a diabolical female in lieu of a male villain. After Eric defeats Ursula, King Triton is restored to power and her former prisoners are released. Thus, Eric fulfills his role as heroic rescuer by saving the woman he loves and the merkingdom from danger, and thus a relationship is constructed between a strong, invulnerable heroic protector and weak, vulnerable victims (Ariel and the kingdom). In this narrative, Ariel and the merworld are subordinate to Eric because they submit to and thus are entirely dependent on Eric's role as their guardian (Messerschmidt 2010, 112). In another sense, as Ariel articulates a desire to leave the merworld, Eric also recues her from an ordinary life. By leaving the ocean, Ariel becomes completely dependent on Eric and this unequal relationship is sanctioned by the institution of heterosexual marriage.

Ursula: Subordinate Oppositional Femininity

Ursula clearly subverts many aspects of dominant femininity and for this reason can be seen as a representation of oppositional femininity. In terms of physical appearance, she is not conventionally beautiful, older, and appears unconcerned about being overweight. Ursula's corpulent body stands in sharp contrast to Ariel's carefully sculpted body, which reflects self-control and discipline and exemplifies dominant femininity.

Ursula's sexuality emerges in the form of Vanessa. The fact that Ursula has to transform herself into Vanessa in order to sexually entice Eric reflects the cultural stigmatization toward women whose bodies do not conform to the confines of dominant femininity. As indicated, the portrayal of Vanessa as a calculating seductress reflects a culturally marginalized whore image who exemplifies an oppositional form of femininity.

More significantly, Ursula reflects a deeper and more disturbing cultural stereotype of a power-hungry female who uses covert tactics to accomplish her goals. Ursula uses deception to lure Eric away from Ariel, so she can achieve her ultimate aspiration of dethroning King Triton and ruling over the sea. Ursula embodies the cultural stereotype of an overly ambitious woman who wields power for a limited period of time but is eventually rendered powerless by a man. Significantly, Ursula is the only powerful female figure in the film and clearly is a negative representation of a powerful woman.

Ursula is both subordinate to Ariel's dominant form of femininity and subordinated by Eric's dominant form of masculinity. As I discussed above, Ursula's appearance, age, and weight stand in sharp contrast to Ariel's. Whereas Ariel is thin, young, beautiful, and sexually desirable, Ursula is overweight, old, ugly, and sexually undesirable. Over the course of the film, Ariel does not sub-ordinate Ursula to reconfirm her dominant femininity but the power-hungry Ursula is eventually disempowered by Eric. While Ursula clearly subverts many aspects of dominant femininity, her biggest transgressions are her over-confidence and overambitiousness, thus she is quickly sanctioned.

Beauty and the Beast

Beauty and the Beast opens with a narrative about a vain young prince who rejects an old beggar woman's offer to exchange a rose for a night's shelter. The beggar woman then reveals her true identity as a beautiful enchantress. Convinced of his coldheartedness, she places a curse on the young man which transforms him into a monstrous beast. In order to break the curse, he must learn to love and be loved by another prior to his twenty-first birthday. The Beast retreats into a reclusive existence within the confines of his castle.

Belle, the film's protagonist, resides in a provincial French village where others view her as peculiar due to her interest in books, her self-confidence, and her apparent disinterest in romance. Her oddity becomes even more pronounced when she rejects the hypermasculine Gaston's offer of marriage, whose vanity, exemplary physique, and self-confidence make him both a heartthrob and local hero. Belle's father, Maurice, an eccentric inventor, does not pressure Belle to conform to social norms but assures her that his latest invention will improve their lives.

Maurice departs for an invention fair but gets lost along the way and seeks refuge in the Beast's castle. The Beast is far from hospitable toward Maurice and imprisons him in the castle dungeon. Maurice appears doomed to eternal entrapment since no one knows of his whereabouts.

Fortunately, Belle goes searching for her father and eventually finds him. The Beast, however, is enraged when he finds Belle in the tower dungeon with her father. Belle altruistically offers to sacrifice her own freedom in exchange for her father's. Despite Maurice's objections, the Beast accepts the offer, and Maurice is immediately released and escorted out of the castle.

After adjusting to her new life in the Beast's castle, Belle and the Beast pre dictably appear to possess romantic feelings for each other. The Beast gradu-ally becomes able to control his volatile temper, and Belle instructs him in the intricacies of social etiquette, ballroom dancing, and anger management. De-spite the Beast's apparent amorous feelings toward Belle, he recognizes her melancholy and Belle confesses that she misses her father. The Beast releases Belle from her vow to remain in the castle and she returns to the village.

Following a series of events, Gaston leads a mob to the Beast's castle. Gas-ton enters the castle in search of the Beast and to his amazement finds a broken figure, not a terrifying monster. Gaston attacks the Beast and thrusts them both onto the rooftop, but the Beast is unresponsive to Gaston's provocations. However, the Beast regains his will to live when Belle reappears and he begins to fight with Gaston. The duel ends with Gaston stabbing and seriously wounding the Beast but falling from the roof in the process. Belle quickly rushes to the side of the dying Beast and declares her love for him which simultaneously breaks the spell and revives him. The narrative ends with Belle and the handsome prince dancing.

Gender in Beauty and the Beast

In contrast to Ariel, Belle can be seen as embodying a hybrid form of femininity, which both accommodates and resists dominant femininity. I will demonstrate how elements of Belle's character reflect feminist notions of gender equality; however, the predominant representation of Belle is as a woman who is ultimately fulfilled by heterosexual romance.

Physical Appearance   Much like Ariel, Belle's attractive, slim body can be seen as a prototype of dominant femininity. Gaston even proclaims that she is the most beautiful girl in the village. However, Disney also emphasizes Belle's independence and intelligence, which are characteristics atypically associated with dominant femininity, thus making her a more complex character than to Ariel. Also in contrast to *The Little Mermaid*, physical appearance is apparently a nonsalient feature in Belle and the Beast's relationship. This is partly attributable to the Beast's hideous demeanor and subsequent inability to be concerned about his partner's appearance. More significantly, the film appears to be relaying a broader, more positive message that inner beauty matters most.

Sexuality   Belle's conservative style of dress, lack of makeup, and disinterest in romance together construct a conservative sexual demeanor. The virgin/whore dichotomy emerges much more subtly in this film as a contrast between the intelligent, thin, virgin-like Belle and other young women who are dimwitted, voluptuous, and single-mindedly infatuated with Gaston. Their sexually revealing style of dress indexes a more provocative sexuality than Belle's and thus can be read as a reflection of the virgin/whore dichotomy. Conceivably, Gaston would engage in casual sexual encounters with these women; however, he notably rejects them and desires Belle as his future wife. Despite Belle's intelligence and independence, which could conceivably threaten his masculine ego, Belle's beauty and virgin-like demeanor are apparently sufficient criteria to qualify her as the primary candidate for his future wife.

Self-Confidence   Belle expresses a certain degree of self-confidence which contests notions of dominant femininity. Most likely, women who lived in eighteenth-century provincial France faced pressure to marry by a certain age and overconfidence decreased their value on the marriage market. Belle, by contrast, appears unconcerned about her single status. Nonetheless, her goal to leave this provincial village is rendered inconsequential at the end of the film when she marries a charming prince. This is an example of how Disney incorporates a modern notion such as that of an independent woman which appears to subvert dominant femininity, but reconstitutes dominant femininity through defining Belle's personal fulfillment through supporting the transformation of the Beast into a refined prince and ultimately a romantic relationship.

My discussion of Belle illustrates she is both archetype and antithesis of dominant femininity. Belle's physical beauty and virginal sexuality make her a paradigm of dominant femininity, yet her bookishness, independence, and desire to leave her hometown oppose conventional feminine practices. By both embodying and resisting norms of dominant femininity, Belle constructs a dominant oppositional femininity.

Belle does not practice hegemonic femininity because she refuses to form a compliant and accommodating subordinate relationship with Gaston and thus submit to his authority. In contrast to the other single townswomen, who are completely infatuated with Gaston, Belle regards him as egotistical and narcissistic. Belle's rejection of Gaston and the sexism he represents is most apparent when she declines his marriage proposal. In the proposal scene, Gaston assures Belle that they will have many male children and that she will oversee their upbringing. Thus, Belle is not only rejecting Gaston but also a patriarchal conjugal relationship where wives uncontestably submit to their husband's authority. In contrast, Belle apparently desires a domestic partnership that is built upon mutual respect and equality.

Gaston simultaneously practices a dominant and hegemonic form of masculinity. He embodies a macho form of dominant masculinity due to his exemplary physical strength, attractiveness, self-confidence, aggression, and pronounced heterosexuality. At the same time, he enacts hegemonic masculinity by establishing a hierarchical relationship with other men and women. For example, he frequently bullies Lefou, his loyal sidekick, and constructs himself as superior to the Beast. In relation to Belle, Gaston automatically presumes she will accept his marriage proposal and then occupy a traditional domestic role. After Belle declines, Gaston devises a plan to have her father committed to a mental institution unless she reconsiders his offer. Once again Gaston attempts to coerce Belle into accepting his offer through using his social connections and material wealth to bribe a psychiatrist to declare Maurice insane.

The film also portrays a subordinate oppositional masculinity through the Beast. Similar to Gaston, the Beast is physically strong, heterosexual, and aggressive prior to Belle's reformative efforts. In contrast to Gaston, however, the

Beast is also unattractive, insecure, compassionate, and nonviolent. The Beast's subordinate status mostly stems from his physical appearance which inhibits him from forming heterosexual relationships and thus engaging a dominant form of masculinity. Simultaneously, practicing nonviolence, lacking confidence, and exhibiting compassion are atypical masculine practices, thus the Beast can be seen as opposing both dominant masculinity and the hierarchical relationship between men and women, masculinity and femininity.

Although Belle's rejection of Gaston and hegemonic masculinity and preference for a relationship with the Beast can be read as a progressive gender representation, the film's conventional narrative development and closure nullify any subversive potential. As the film progresses Belle's desire to leave this provincial town is gradually consumed by her central role in civilizing the Beast, which she apparently enjoys. Thus, Belle's central role in this film is to educate the Beast on the intricacies of social etiquette and ultimately support his transformation into a refined gentleman. In the end, this is not a narrative about an independent woman pursuing her own ambitions, but one about a woman whose life is rendered meaningful through a heterosexual relationship. This same theme surfaced in *The Little Mermaid*.

Pocahontas

Pocahontas is very loosely based upon the actual events of an early encounter between Native American Indians and European settlers. In the film, Pocahontas is the free-spirited daughter of Chief Powhatan who wishes for her to marry the serious, but respected, warrior Kocoum. Pocahontas, however, is unsure about this union and, similar to *The Little Mermaid* and *Beauty and the Beast*, appears to desire a life outside her village. Her apprehensions are further confirmed by a dream about a spinning arrow which suggests that her destiny may lie elsewhere. In an attempt to resolve her dilemma, Pocahontas seeks the advice of Grandmother Willow, a talking tree spirit, who advises her to follow her heart.

While Pocahontas is struggling to come to grips with her destiny, a group of English settlers land in the New World with the intention of excavating gold. The greedy Governor John Ratcliffe is the leader of this expedition and the film's protagonist, Captain John Smith, is a member of the expedition.

On Ratcliffe's orders, Smith is digging for gold when he encounters Pocahontas and is immediately enchanted by her. Secretly, Smith and Pocahontas become acquainted, and she teaches him that her people are not *savages* but possess a deep reverence for nature and a sophisticated culture. Predictably, they fall in love but never actually become romantically involved. In a refreshing change from *The Little Mermaid* and *Beauty and the Beast*, the budding romance between Smith and Pocahontas does not attain prime importance in the film but is superseded by the more critical mission of making Ratcliffe understand that the land is devoid of gold and therefore he should abandon his expedition.

A misunderstanding causes one of the settlers to kill Kocoum, and feelings of animosity escalate between the Native Americans and English. Smith altruistically accepts the blame for Kocoum's death, is captured, and sentenced to death. Ratcliffe uses Smith's sentence to justify a declaration of war against the Native Americans, and the settlers proceed to the Native American village where Smith is about to be executed. In a climactic scene, Powhatan is about to execute Smith when Pocahontas throws herself in front of him, declaring her love, and asks both sides to consider where their path of hatred has led them. Chief Powhatan responds by releasing John Smith. Nonetheless, an enraged Ratcliffe proceeds to fire a gun at Chief Powhatan, whom Smith pushes aside, takes the bullet, and becomes injured in the process. Consequently, Smith must return to England to receive medical treatment.

In contrast to the romantic love narrative espoused by the other films, Smith and Pocahontas do not live happily ever after. At the end of the film, Pocahontas comes to the realization that the spinning arrow symbolized her encounter with John Smith; however, she decides that her destiny lies with her own people in the New World and refuses Smith's offer to accompany him to England. In marked contrast to *The Little Mermaid* and *Beauty and the Beast*, Pocahontas's life was altered by a man but her existence was not entirely defined through heterosexual romance. Compared to the other films, this ending provides a more progressive representation of femininity.

Gender in Pocahontas

Similar to Belle, Pocahontas is a non-prototypically feminine character. However, in spite of possessing some unfeminine qualities, Disney still manages to construct a character who embodies aspects of dominant femininity and overwhelmingly is a nonsubversive representation.

Physical Appearance   In spite of Pocahontas's subversive qualities, her beauty and ethnic exoticness form the basis of Smith's initial attraction to her. Exemplifying the Disney prototype, she has a slim figure, large eyes, and could be considered beautiful. However, she is also represented as intelligent, independent, and searching for a destiny outside the boundaries of her tribal village. Concomitantly, Disney can be seen as subverting dominant femininity by presenting her as social nonconformist but reaffirming dominant femininity by foregrounding the importance of women's appearance on the heterosexual market.

Sexuality   Sexuality is a nonsalient component of this film. Unlike *The Little Mermaid* and *Beauty and the Beast*, the virgin/whore dichotomy is not strikingly apparent. As the story develops, it is apparent that Pocahontas and Smith are in love. However, Smith's increased understanding of and respect for Native American culture and attempts to reduce intolerance and create mutual understanding between the white settlers and Native American Indians are more prevalent themes. We also need to remember that the film is inspired by actual historical events and that Smith and Pocahontas apparently were never lovers, which could be the main reason why the romance never develops in the film. Moreover, although the film is historically faithful to the absence of a romantic relationship between Pocahontas and Smith, Giroux (2010, 107) importantly points out how the film also disturbingly glosses over the environmental destruction, disease, and genocide brought on by Western colonialism. Therefore, I am unconvinced the absence of a romance between Smith and Pocahontas is Disney's attempt to offer an alternative to a narrative of heterosexual romance, but quite conceivably Disney's loose rendition of historical events.

Self-Confidence   Pocahontas also subverts dominant femininity by exhibiting a degree of self-confidence. A central theme in the first part of the movie is Pocahontas's contention that her destiny may lie outside the traditional life trajectory of marriage and presumably motherhood. At the end of the film, she also exhibits self-confidence by refusing Smith's offer to accompany him back to England and proclaiming that her destiny lies in the New World.

Alternatively, the film is not a young woman's coming-of-age story, but, similar to *Beauty and the Beast*, is the story of a woman who is defined through supporting the transformation of a man. The early part of the film portrays Pocahontas's struggle over accepting an arranged marriage and conforming to social norms or following an alternative path, symbolized by the spinning arrow. As the film progresses, however, Pocahontas is increasingly and primarily defined through her relationship with and eventual rescue of John Smith (Giroux 2010, 107). Therefore, *Pocahontas* can be interpreted as the story of a woman who facilitates Smith's transformation from an ethnocentric racist to a diplomatic ambassador who is set on creating alliances between Europe and the New World.

The forms of masculinity and femininity practiced by John Smith and Pocahontas do not establish and maintain a hierarchical and complementary relationship; thus neither embodies hegemonic masculinity nor hegemonic femininity. John Smith's superior physique, self-confidence, and presumed heterosexuality make him an exemplar of dominant masculinity; however, he does not construct hierarchical relationships between other men and women. On the contrary, through his relationship with Pocahontas, he gains a better understanding of and tolerance for Native American Indian culture, which prompts him to resist Ratcliffe's colonial conquest. Thus, he resists the masculine practice of subordinating Native American men and women and in the process embracing a hegemonic form of masculinity.

Smith's dominant form of masculinity is complemented by Pocahontas's dominant femininity. Pocahontas's dominant femininity is suggested by her physical appearance and virgin-like sexuality. Similar to Ariel and Belle, she also possesses a certain degree of self-confidence but she is never overconfident to an extent which would threaten masculine pride and thus render her gender deviant. Far from forming a relationship of compliance and submission with Smith, Pocahontas never hesitates to challenge Smith's racist assumptions about her people and educate him. As I indicated, Pocahontas's relationship with Smith significantly impacted her life; however, unlike both Ariel and Belle, her life is not entirely defined through a heterosexual relationship, so we might read this film as presenting a more progressive representation of femininity.

Mulan

Mulan opens with rebel forces, the Huns, invading China. This impending threat prompts the Emperor to issue an edict which requires a male from every household to join the army.

The story then shifts to focus on Fa Mulan, a young unmarried woman, who is preparing to meet a matchmaker who will hopefully introduce a suitable marriage partner and allow her to bestow honor on her family through marriage. Unfortunately, Mulan makes an unfavorable impression on the matchmaker and thus her matrimonial prospects appear bleak. Once Mulan returns home, her father, Fa Zhou, comforts his disheartened daughter, which is followed by a visit from the imperial army and the issuance of a conscription decree.

Since Fa Zhou is the only male family member, he feels compelled to serve his country and decides to enlist in the army. Mulan contradicts a norm of obedient daughter and objects to her father's enlistment on the basis of his age and an old war-induced injury which has left him with a limp.

In what can be seen as an act of filial piety, Mulan disguises herself as a man, adopts the pseudonym Ping, and decides to enlist in the army. Mulan joins a troop of inexperienced soldiers led by Captain Li Shang, who is unimpressed with their unpreparedness and subjects the troops to a grueling training schedule to condition them for battle. The rigorous training regime appears to create bonds of solidarity among the enlisted soldiers.

The soldiers are presented with an opportunity to demonstrate their newly acquired battle skills in an unprecedented attack by and resulting skirmish with the Huns. Mulan is the heroine of this battle as she fires a cannon which prompts an avalanche that buries the Huns. She also saves Captain Shang but is critically injured in the process. Much to Mulan's dismay, her true identity is discovered when undergoing medical treatment and Shang subsequently discharges her from the military and leads the regiment back to the Imperial City. As Mulan is about to return home, some of the Huns emerge from the snow and set out for the Imperial City. She quickly changes her mind about going home and decides to follow the enemy troop.

Mulan returns to the Imperial City and attempts to warn Shang that rebel forces are inside the Imperial City, but he dismisses her warning largely due to her gender. Thus, we see the dissemination of a cultural stereotype which positions women as ignorant about national security issues. The Emperor is subsequently kidnapped by the Huns; however, Mulan designs and mobilizes a clever plot which results in his successful rescue and she is elevated to the status of heroine.

The Emperor is once again restored to power and bestows Mulan the gifts of his crest and a fallen enemy's sword, and offers her a prestigious position in his cabinet. Although Mulan acknowledges the magnitude of this honor, she declines and expresses a desire to return home.

Resembling the successful completion of a hero's (heroine's) journey and again representing an act of filial piety, Mulan returns home and presents the Emperor's gifts to her father. She expects to be reprimanded by her father, but instead he throws the gifts aside and proclaims that she is the most precious gift of all. Apparently, Mulan also made a lasting impression on Captain Shang as he arrives at her house and is invited to stay for dinner. The movie ends with Mulan's grandmother enthusiastically proclaiming that she wants to sign up for the next war, ostensibly as an opportunity to meet Mr. Right.

Gender in Mulan

Among Ariel, Belle, and Pocahontas, Mulan appears to resist many practices which comprise dominant femininity and thus initially appears to offer a more progressive representation of femininity. However, I will demonstrate that while Mulan does indeed contest key elements of dominant femininity, she is nevertheless feminized in significant ways in the film which effectively nullifies the subversive potential of those qualities. Rather than constructing a story about a heroine who challenges dominant femininity and ultimately saves China, Disney's ending suggests that despite the significance of women's accomplishments, they remain incomplete without a stable heterosexual romance.

Physical Appearance   Paralleling the other films, Mulan is both beautiful and thin; however, Disney does not overemphasize Mulan's appearance but instead foregrounds her difficulties conforming to conventional notions of femininity, which potentially enable her to embody masculinity more easily than a conventionally feminine character. For example, Mulan is depicted as both ungraceful and indecorous in a scene where she meets the matchmaker, which can be seen as a nontraditional representation of femininity. Presumably, it is easier for the audience to image a character such as Mulan successfully cross-dressing and enlisting in the military than a more stereotypical feminine one such as Ariel.

In spite of Mulan's apparent difficulties with aligning her embodied social actions with norms constituting dominant femininity, she is never portrayed as completely masculine. In contrast to the male soldiers, for example, Mulan (Ping) is depicted as concerned with personal hygiene. In another scene, Ping is the only soldier who expresses condolences to Captain Shang over his father's death. Therefore, Ping's expression of emotion contradicts the masculine stereotype of emotional reticence (Cameron 2007, 11; Connell 2009, 60). Although Mulan is depicted as unconventionally feminine, she is never represented as completely unfeminine.

Sexuality Mainly owing to Mulan's attempt to pass as a man, her sexuality is largely underemphasized. Near the film's completion, she is nonetheless rendered feminine by the Emperor and Grandma Fa. For instance, the Emperor encourages Shang to visit Mulan's home, complimenting her uniqueness, which suggests that she is a sound marriage candidate. Upon returning home after saving China, Grandma Fa comments that Mulan should have brought home a man, not merely a sword. And then later, when Shang arrives, Grandma Fa articulates her desire to sign up for the next war.

In foregrounding these examples, I am not taking issue with romantic relationships themselves but drawing attention to the fact that in spite of Mulan's tremendous accomplishments, she is still constructed as an incomplete woman. This has been a continual theme in all four of the Disney movies, and I will later demonstrate how this phenomenon is neither unique nor confined to Disney. The problematic nature of an incomplete woman discourse is apparent when we consider the absence of a complementary incomplete man discourse. Eric, the Beast, John Smith, and Shang are neither represented as primarily concerned with nor fulfilled by heterosexual love. Significantly, their primary accomplishments are entirely separate from the arena of heterosexual love. Mulan, by contrast, saves the entire nation, but her grandmother apparently regards her relationship with Shang as her greatest achievement.

Self-Confidence Of the discussed movies, I would argue that *Mulan* offers the most progressive representation of a self-confident woman. Unlike the other movies, Mulan's self-confidence is removed from the arena of heterosexual love. Mulan expresses self-confidence in her ability to pass as a male soldier and bestow honor on her family. In fact, Mulan is shown as displaying great resolve in making many of her decisions. For example, Mulan confidently decides to fire a cannon that causes an avalanche, temporarily immobilizing the Huns. In addition, Mulan is represented as confident when she returns to the Imperial City to warn Shang about the Huns, and once again when she devises a clever plot to foil the Huns once they overtake the Emperor. In the scene where the Emperor offers her a position in his cabinet, she can also be seen as possessing great resolve when she refuses his offer, which could potentially cause an affront, and articulates a strong desire to return home.

This movie also nicely depicts the gendered nature of filial piety and honor. At the onset of the film, filial piety and bestowing honor on one's family are depicted as involving marriage for women and military service for men. Mulan's despair over her inability to impress the matchmaker is understandable given that marriage is the primary means through which daughters bring honor on their families. Since Fa Zhou is without sons, the only way to bring honor to his family is for him to enlist. Conceivably, using his disability as a reason to refuse the conscription notice would shame his family and potentially emasculate him.

Given the gendered nature of both honor and filial piety, Mulan stretches the boundaries imposed by gender through military enlistment, but she does not completely subvert dominant femininity. As Mulan was unable to bring honor on her family through the traditional channel of marriage, she challenged notions of femininity and bestowed honor on her family in a conventionally masculine manner. Nonetheless, the salience of an incomplete woman discourse in this movie effectively feminized the conventionally unfeminine Mulan.

Mulan and Shang offer representations of a dominant form of masculinity and dominant oppositional femininity. Shang is not only physically strong, self-confident, and heterosexual, but also a military hero. Although Shang uses violence and physical force to defeat his enemies, he does not establish a hierarchical relationship of dominance and submission with Mulan or other women in the film and therefore cannot be viewed as embodying hegemonic masculinity.

Mulan both embodies and explicitly resists central practices comprising dominant femininity. Although Mulan is beautiful and thin, she also possesses physical strength and self-confidence. Most obviously, Mulan's cross-dressing and military service subvert notions of dominant femininity. Thus, Mulan draws on the typically masculine resource of physical prowess to construct her gender identity. In addition, Mulan also saves Captain Shang from the Huns and eventually plays a crucial role in the defeat of the Huns and the heroic rescue of the Emperor. Departing from a traditional masculine hero narrative, Mulan is the heroic protector who rescues China from the villain-ous Huns. Although Mulan opposes many practices associated with dominant femininity, she is ultimately represented as a woman whose life is completed by heterosexual romance and marriage.

Discussion

A disturbing and prevalent theme common to all of these films is a represen-tation of women as incomplete without heterosexual romance and the subse-quent normalization of a heteronormative gender order. Not only do these films privilege heterosexuality but also monogamy, a virginal representation of female sexuality, the social institution of marriage, and a narrow conceptu-alization of beauty, which collectively underpin and stabilize a heteronorma-tive social order. Neither Ariel nor Belle fit into their respective societies; however, their personal dissatisfaction was eventually deemphasized and in-stead their desire to enter into a heterosexual relationship was foregrounded. Similarly, Pocahontas was initially constructed as a gender rebel who was uninterested in an arranged marriage and accompanying domesticity. Poca-hontas's rebelliousness was soon forgotten as she too became single-mindedly focused on capturing John Smith's heart. Mulan is also represented as a social nonconformist who resists aspects of dominant femininity, but by the end of the movie she exemplifies the Disney model of a woman who is completed by heterosexual love. In short, the films do not offer progressive representations of female protagonists, but instead sustain archaic representations of female characters as incomplete until they get married. These films illustrate how media representations can simultaneously subvert and reify traditional gen-der representations and ultimately disseminate conventional gender images which contribute to stabilizing a patriarchal gender order.

The next sections of the chapter focus on representations of femininity in *Fatal Attraction, Bridget Jones's Diary* (hereafter *BJD*), and *Sex and the City* (hereafter *SATC*). As these films simultaneously inculcate and resist tradi-tional notions of femininity, the characters' relationship with dominant femininity is somewhat ambiguous. However, this ambivalence is precisely how gendered media representations manage to survive in a post-feminist era of presupposed gender equality.

Single Women

Prior to conducting an analysis of the aforementioned films, I will first criti-cally review some previous research on single women. Although film and television disseminate fictitious gendered images, nevertheless I have also indicated how the media is a key site where gender is not merely represented but also constructed. Hence, we can expect to see aspects of reality reflected in these fictitious representations.

Important insights can be gained from an examination of some of the semantic connotations and word collocations related to *single woman*. Collocations refer to "systematic co-occurrences of words, which can often reveal something about connotations or hidden associations which are triggered when we encounter a particular word" (Baker 2008, 28). Although the English language distinguishes between *male bachelors* and *female spinsters*, women can also be referred to as *bachelorettes* (Baker 2008, 203). The nomenclature of *bachelorette* illustrates how female terms derive from male ones, but the reverse case is rare (Baker 2008, 203). In addition, I contend that this phenomenon also indexes the subordinate place femininity occupies vis-à-vis masculinity. This disparity becomes strikingly clear when we examine the word collocations which co-occur with bachelor versus spinster and accompanying semantic connotations.

The existence of the collocation of *eligible bachelor* and absence of *eligible spinster* indicates the social stigmatization of unmarried women. Baker (2008, 204) maintains that eligible bachelors refer to "young (heterosexual) men who are either physically attractive or wealthy and therefore eligible for marriage." Clearly, physical attractiveness and material wealth enhance a man's value on the marriage market, but I would argue that to a large degree age does not diminish a man's value on the marriage market. In support of this interpretation, *People* magazine publishes an annual *50 Most Eligible Bachelors* issue and middle-aged men such as George Clooney have been featured. Similarly, *People* also nominates an annual *Sexiest Man Alive* and a quick glance at the winners from 1985 to the present reveals a wide age range from twenty-seven to fifty-six. Notably, *People* publishes neither a complementary *50 Most Eligible Bachelorettes* nor *Sexiest Woman Alive* issue, which again points to the superior status masculinity occupies in the United States and perhaps elsewhere.

This discussion has not meant to suggest that bachelor is never constructed as a problematic identity. Although I would argue that bachelor never experiences an equivalent level of social denigration as spinster, Baker makes the important point that a bachelor's eligibility also has an expiration date. Based on a corpus analysis, Baker (2008, 207) found that bachelors are also constructed as lonely, victims of crime, and unable to care for themselves. The final description indexes a very traditional and heteronormative view of romantic relationships where men and women are different but complementary and women are responsible for looking after men's daily needs.

The preceding, albeit brief, discussion of bachelor illustrates how the term is not an entirely unproblematic identity; however, I would argue that the positive connotations outweigh the negative ones, which stands in sharp contrast to spinster. For instance, *eligible bachelor* and *lonely spinster* still serve as canonical images in many Western societies (Reynolds 2008, 22), with the latter collocation clearly invoking negative connotations. Furthermore, a spinster is by definition an older woman and therefore past her prime in a culture which idealizes youthful women. Baker (2008, 217) also contends that spinsters are regularly described as "unattractive, plain, sex-starved, or sexually frustrated" and that "compared with bachelors, there is no 'happy young spinster' identity, so the sexual freedom afforded to attached young males is not similarly given to women." Baker's comment about sexual freedom references the previously discussed sexual double standard which condones permissive male sexuality but sanctions female promiscuity.

Prior to analyzing *BJD* and *SATC*, I am going to first examine a notable predecessor: *Fatal Attraction*. This film portrays a professional single woman who is driven to the point of madness due to her obsession with a married man. The film's portrayal of graphic sex caused a strong reaction in the United States upon release. Prior to this film, active female sexuality was not portrayed on the silver screen. Notwithstanding, I will demonstrate how this film is not a positive portrayal of sexually assertive single women, but instead exemplifies a genre of film which pathologizes professionally successful single women. Indeed, Susan Faludi (1992) cites this film as an example of a *backlash* phenomenon where the media disseminate negative images of modern women inhabiting an era of purported gender equality. The backlash is a vitriolic attack against feminism which maintains that modern women are unhappy and desire a return to the traditional values of marriage, motherhood, and full-time domesticity. *Fatal Attraction's* protagonist represents a professionally successful single woman who has reaped the benefits of feminism yet is still unhappy. As the film espouses an overwhelmingly negative portrayal of a mentally ill single woman, the protagonist can be seen as representing a subordinate oppositional femininity. I analyze the film in terms of which aspects of dominant femininity the protagonist sustains and subverts and again discuss the issue of whether she contributes to sustaining toxic masculine practices or equalizing gender relations.

Fatal Attraction

Fatal Attraction tells the story of how a man's affair with a *psychotic* woman has devastating consequences. Dan Gallagher is a seemingly happily married successful attorney who resides with his family in New York City. Dan and his wife Beth attend a party where he meets Alex Forrest, an editor for a publishing company. The two appear mutually attracted to each other but nothing develops beyond a mild flirtation. Soon after striking up a conversation with Alex, Dan is summoned by Beth and they leave the party.

After they get home, Dan begins to prepare for bed, when Beth reminds him that the dog needs walking. Dan reluctantly walks the dog, and when he returns to the bedroom, their daughter, Ellen, is in bed with Beth. Dan's disappointed expression implies that his plans for a passionate evening of lovemaking have been thwarted and viewers are left with the impression that he is sexually deprived.

The next day Beth takes Ellen to her parents' house for the weekend, but Dan has to stay in Manhattan and work. Coincidentally, Alex and Dan attend the same meeting, so they are briefly reacquainted. Once again, nothing develops beyond a mild flirtation within the context of work, but their mutual attraction to each other is obvious.

After leaving the office, Dan gets caught in the middle of a rainstorm with a broken umbrella. Alex, who is coincidentally nearby, offers to share her umbrella, and Dan suggests they get a drink. A drink turns into dinner and before long they are flirting. Notably, Dan is the one who initiates the date, but Alex decides that they will have a love affair. Accordingly, Dan assumes the traditional role of male aggressor, but Alex is the temptress who ultimately lures him into marital infidelity. An evening of passionate sex is followed by Dan leaving her apartment early the next morning.

Alex calls Dan the next day and is clearly offended that he left without saying goodbye. Dan attempts to decline her invitation to lunch, but her persistence pays off as he reluctantly consents. They end up spending most of the afternoon together, and Dan attempts to leave in the early evening; however, Alex invites him to stay overnight again since his wife is not due to return until the next day. After Dan declines, Alex slits her wrists in a final attempt to manipulate him to stay longer. Alex was successful as Dan stays with her until she stabilizes, and viewers are provided with an initial glimpse of Alex's mental instability.

Dan attempts to return to the routine of work and family life; however, Alex keeps resurfacing. She appears at his office with tickets to see *Madame Butterfly* and even calls him at home. Dan finally agrees to meet her after she calls him at 2:00 a.m. The next day they meet and Alex discloses to Dan that she is pregnant and intends to raise his child. Alex is clinging to a hope that Dan will take an active role in raising the child, but he wants to sever all ties with her.

While Alex's fatal attraction is developing, the Gallaghers are in the process of preparing to sell their apartment and moving to the suburb of Bedford. As Dan refuses to return Alex's calls, she comes to their apartment under the guise of a potential buyer and is talking with Beth when Dan arrives home. Dan is enraged and goes to Alex's apartment later that night to confront her.

During the confrontation, Alex insists that she will not be ignored and that Dan needs to claim responsibility for his actions.

After the Gallaghers move to Bedford, Alex's obsession with Dan becomes even more pronounced. Alex has a cassette tape delivered to his office which is filled with verbal abuse, stalks him in a parking garage, and follows him home the same night. We see a jealous Alex peering into a window of his house and she soon vomits in the bushes, purportedly sickened by their domestic bliss.

Alex's obsession is portrayed as extreme when the Gallagher family is visiting Beth's parents in the country. Beth, Dan, and Ellen return home to find the family rabbit boiling on the stove, which prompts Dan to disclose his affair to Beth, who is understandably furious. Dan calls Alex and informs her that Beth knows of their relationship, but Alex accuses him of lying. Beth then gets on the phone and warns Alex that if she persists, she will kill her. After the fateful phone conversation, Dan moves to a hotel.

Alex's next psychotic act is to kidnap Ellen from school and take her to an amusement park. Beth ends up in a car accident in the course of her frantic search for Ellen, whom Alex brings home at the end of the day. Beth is briefly hospitalized but did not sustain serious injuries from the accident, and so she is soon released. Dan later goes to the police, and they promise to bring Alex in for questioning; however, they later call him to say that she is missing.

Beth has apparently forgiven Dan as he has moved back home and is caring for her. Dan is downstairs fixing Beth tea while she is taking a bath. Alex appears in the bathroom with a knife. Alex attacks Beth with a butcher's knife, and Dan races upstairs to save her. Dan pushes Alex into the bathtub, seemingly drowning her, but she comes back to life and Beth shoots and instantaneously kills her. The film ends with a close-up of a family portrait, which implies that the evil temptress/witch has been expunged from their house.

Gender in Fatal Attraction

It might be an overstatement to claim that Dan legitimizes a hierarchical relationship between men and women, masculinity and femininity, and therefore represents hegemonic masculinity; nonetheless, aspects of his masculinity can be considered hegemonic. Dan embodies a class-based form of dominant *transnational business (lawyer) masculinity*, which can also be hegemonic. Since the film is set in a time prior to the onset of globalization, *national lawyer masculinity* might be a more appropriate term. Transnational business masculinity is underpinned by the gender practices of exerting authority, social conservatism, compulsory heterosexuality, and subscribing to a strong family division of labor (Connell and Wood 2005, 348). Reflecting these practices, Dan can exercise authority at work and naturalizes a conventional division of labor with his wife. Transnational business masculinity can also be marked by a libertarian sexuality, which is reflected by Dan's extramarital affair (Connell 2000, 52). Nowhere in the film is there any evidence which specifically indicates that Dan establishes and maintains hierarchical relationships with other men and women; nevertheless, his competitiveness at work, domestic noninvolvement, sexual infidelity, and disregard for Alex's feelings are practices which establish and maintain unequal relationships between men and women, masculinity and femininity. Therefore, I would characterize him as practicing a dominant form of masculinity with hegemonic components, which illustrates how individuals can simultaneously practice two forms of masculinity or femininity.

Beth's dominant femininity forms a complementary but not hierarchical relationship with Dan's dominant masculinity. Although Beth could be considered subordinate in the sense that she is financially dependent upon Dan, the film never suggests that Beth desires to enter the labor force. Thus, Beth practices a suburban housewife form of dominant femininity which is characterized by sexual fidelity, motherhood, and complete devotion to her family. In the context of the 1980s, Beth's dominant femininity is superior to Alex's dominant oppositional femininity because Beth has acquired the feminine capital of marriage, family, and a middle-class lifestyle.

Alex Forrest: Subordinate Oppositional Femininity

The dominant forms of masculinity and femininity practiced by Dan and Beth stand in sharp contrast to Alex's subordinate oppositional femininity. Collectively, Alex's singleness, sexual promiscuity, childlessness, and professional success are gender practices which refuse to accommodate hegemonic masculinity in a relationship of subordination and thus oppose hegemonic gender relations. Although Alex does indeed embody the dominant feminine characteristics of physical beauty and fitness, the above-mentioned practices stand in sharp contrast and are subordinate to Beth's conservative sexuality, married status, and total devotion to her family. Furthermore, Alex embodies a subordinate oppositional femininity because her permissive sexuality marks her as a *slut*. A slut represents an oppositional femininity for refusing to form a complementary and subordinate relationship with hegemonic masculinity and is subordinate to certain dominant femininities for transgressing a norm of relationship-oriented passive female sexuality (Messerschmidt forthcoming, 32).

In a similar vein with the Disney films analyzed, the dominant narrative disseminated by *Fatal Attraction* is that women desire monogamous heterosexual relationships. Unlike the Disney heroines, however, Alex did not spend her youth searching for true love but pursued a career and engaged in casual sexual encounters, which she eventually regrets. Although Dan and Alex spend a weekend engaged in mutually consensual passionate sex, Alex's desire for commitment and Dan's presumption that the relationship was short-term reflect essentialist notions that women are relationship-oriented and men are sexual predators. Alex's desire for a family is further confirmed when she tells Dan that she is pregnant and intends to have his child. The predominant message conveyed by the film is that women who wait too long to marry and start a family may have few options in middle-age and accordingly have to settle for an undesirable situation like Alex, who is desperately clinging to a relationship with a married family man. Despite Alex's opposition to many elements of dominant femininity, viewers are left with a strong impression that she covets Beth's middle-class domestic lifestyle and thus desires to practice a dominant form of femininity.

Representations of Single Women

The dominant representation of single women in *Fatal Attraction* is that they threaten the sanctity of heterosexual nuclear families. The Gallaghers were a happy family until Alex entered their lives and attempted to destroy their middle-class bliss. Thus, married women should be wary of single women for the threat they pose to the stability of their relationships. Reynolds (2008, 54) conducted interviews with single women and discovered that some participants expressed feelings of social exclusion over their non-single friends' insecurities about the purported threat single women pose to monogamous couples. Accordingly, we see evidence of a notion suggesting that non-single women should be wary of the potential threat single women pose to the stability of their committed romantic relationships or a *women beware women* discourse (Sunderland 2004, 90).

Most problematically, *Fatal Attraction* portrays the gradual unraveling of a successful professional woman into a woman driven mad by her psychotic fixation with a man. When Dan and Alex meet at work, she is portrayed as a self-confident working professional; however, as the film progresses her obsession with heterosexual love overshadows all other aspects of her identity. After the initial meeting where she is reacquainted with Dan, there are no other scenes which even suggest that she has a career. A valid question arises as to how she has time to continually pursue Dan if she has a full-time career. In the course of the film, Alex is simultaneously feminized by her desire for a man's love and demonized by the threat she poses to the stability of his family.

Oppositional Femininities' Role in Troubling Gender Relations

Alex both challenges and reaffirms emotional relations. Her *perverse* sexuality challenges an ideology of passive female sexuality; however, her inability to separate casual sex from emotional attachment ultimately portrays her as a stereotypical woman. While Dan can easily engage with the permissive discourse, Alex's emotions and perhaps femaleness prevent her from engaging in the same behavior. At the same time, the portrayal of a woman with a sexual desire who is lonely, obsessive, and pathological serves to stigmatize women with a permissive sexuality and thus accentuate the virgin/whore dichotomy. Alex stands in sharp contrast to Beth, who is seemingly devoid of sexual desire and thus an exemplary model of a middle-class homemaker dominant femininity.

I would like to suggest that although Alex subverts elements of dominant femininity, her character does not trouble or challenge heteronormative gender relations which position men and women as complementary opposites and thus provide women with a politics of resistance. In this film, the consequences of professional success and singlehood involve eventually realizing that you desire marriage and a family, confirming Faludi's backlash hypothesis. For Alex, who is in her mid-thirties, this pregnancy may be her last chance at motherhood. *Fatal Attraction* takes this one step further and portrays a single woman as willing to go to extreme lengths in order to achieve these goals. The message we are left with is that while feminism has provided women with access to financial independence and professional success, women who exist outside the purportedly oppressive social institutions of marriage and motherhood are somehow incomplete or unfulfilled. Arguably, Alex's character does not contribute to the formation of crisis tendencies in gender relations but her psychotic behavior normalizes a life cycle privileging marriage and full-time motherhood.

Now that I have discussed some of the pervasive social images of single women and analyzed *Fatal Attraction*, I next turn to an analysis of *Bridget Jones's Diary* and later *Sex and the City*. One might hypothesize that since this film and television series were produced somewhat recently, they would portray positive images of single women. Although they do offer some progressive representations of single women, they notably reflect some of the discussed dominant cultural images that denigrate singlehood, which indicates the existence of powerful cultural templates that stigmatize permanently single women. This is partly attributable to cultural norms which associate independence with maleness and dependence with femaleness (Reynolds 2008, 37–38).

My analysis of these media texts is not confined to representations of dominant, hegemonic, subordinate, and oppositional femininities. As these media texts focus on single women, the heroines represent oppositional femininities. In each text, I identified the prevalent themes and thus dominant representations of single women and also present two case studies of women who are representations of oppositional femininities in *SATC*.

Bridget Jones's Diary

Bridget Jones's Diary chronicles the life of an unmarried woman and her friends who inhabit London in the 1990s. The film opens with Bridget embarking on a self-improvement regime as part of a New Year's resolution where she vows to lose weight, quit smoking, reduce her alcohol consumption, develop inner poise, and find a decent man. Notably, these goals are interrelated because a thin body most likely will increase Bridget's marketability on the heterosexual market.

Heterosexual romance becomes Bridget's primary goal throughout the film. Bridget initially falls for a notorious playboy, Daniel Cleaver; however, she eventually ends the relationship once she learns of his propensity for infidelity. After breaking up with Cleaver, Jones reembarks on a self-improvement regime which includes losing weight and pursuing a new career. Nonetheless, the pursuit of heterosexual romance apparently overshadows her career ambitions as Bridget enters a relationship with Mark Darcy. Although the monogamous Mark Darcy represents a sharp contrast to Daniel Cleaver, Bridget is notably portrayed as placing utmost importance on self-improvement for the sake of a heterosexual romance and not personal well-being. Similar to the Disney films analyzed, we see a representation of single women as fulfilled by and thus incomplete without long-term heterosexual relationships.

BJD encompasses a number of contradictory themes related to normative expectations of femininity and representations of a single lifestyle. The film can be seen as subversive as it is ironizing rigid cultural standards constituting heterosexual femininity. On the other hand, the centrality of heterosexual romance in women's lives is neither questioned nor problematized. Viewed from this perspective, *BJD* is arguably not subversive but reaffirms heterosexual love as a primary component of heterosexual femininity. I next examine three prevalent themes which surface in *BJD*: physical appearance, nonheteronormative conceptualizations of family, and representations of single women.

Physical Appearance

The social mandate that women continually modify their bodies in order to conform to rigid notions of heterosexual femininity is a prevalent theme in *BJD*. Bridget's body is represented as dysmorphic, thus requiring vigilant self-regulation and modification through diet and exercise. From the film's onset, we see Bridget painstakingly recording her weight and religiously monitoring her caloric consumption. Disturbingly, Bridget's quest for self-improvement is not for personal wellness but oriented toward increasing her heterosexual desirability. Bridget's self-scrutiny and insecurities reflect the problematic cultural norm that women's physical appearance is their prime source of investable capital on the heterosexual market while men's value fluctuates according to, and thus is contingent upon, their personal accomplishments.

One interpretation of Bridget's fixation with her body is that the film is satirizing social norms which encourage women to embark on a regime of self-surveillance and regulation (Gill 2007, 229). Bridget indeed exemplifies how the embodiment of society's notions of dominant femininity is a never-ending process of bodily maintenance and self-control, which can meet others' criticism when neglected (Whelehan 2002, 48–49). In an early scene, for example, Bridget's mother asks her how she expects to land a man in what she is wearing. As Whelehan (2002, 47–48) has suggested, Bridget walks a thin line between representing average women's normal obsession with their body image and those who develop eating disorders. Bridget's personal insecurities and struggle with weight control arguably reflect social pressures which encourage women to conform to unrealistic ideals of physical perfection that constitute dominant femininity.

Challenging Heteronormative Conceptualizations of Family

A second prevalent theme in *BJD* is challenging heteronormativity by expanding cultural norms which define nuclear families as the only legitimate form of family. In *BJD*, Bridget has an amiable relationship with her parents, who inhabit a suburb of London; however, her most intimate relationships are with close friends. This phenomenon is potentially attributable to a social trend where singles are migrating from the suburbs to the city. As a result, singles who potentially face feelings of loneliness and isolation form alternative families with intimate friends. Irrespective of the cause of this expanded notion of family, *BJD* can be seen as challenging the hegemony of heteronormative nuclear families and providing alternative representations of family.

Representations of Single Women

A third and perhaps overriding theme in *BJD* is representations of single women. Bridget's coinage of the term *singleton*, which she contrasts with *smug marrieds*, can be seen as a positive representation of a single lifestyle. Notably, however, Bridget embarks on an incessant quest to find and marry a perfect man which neutralizes the positive connotations of singleton. One might wonder why Bridget is so eager to enter a relationship if single life is so fulfilling. Contradictions such as this emerge in the film and suggest that permanent singlehood is still a marked social trend in a society which defines marriage and parenthood as milestones definitive of a normative life cycle.

A fairytale type rescue narrative is another theme circulating in *BJD*. In a post-feminist era where women can acquire a degree of professional success and arguably personal fulfillment, *BJD* portrays Bridget as continually pursuing heterosexual romance (Whelehan 2002, 17). In contrast to previous eras, when women's livelihood and social status depended upon marriage, many modern women can lead rich and fulfilling lives without men's financial or emotional support. *BJD* appears to disseminate an ideology which espouses that in spite of the progress made by feminist movements, women still desire to be swept off their feet by a white knight.

BJD offers a very traditional narrative closure where Bridget and Mark Darcy are in a committed relationship. The ending implies that singlehood receives social sanction as a transition period during one's youth; however, long-term relationships and marriage are women's primary goals. Although the film's normalization of long-term heterosexual relationships reflects heternormativity, this is arguably not the most problematic aspect of the ending. I am more troubled by the portrayal of Bridget as overly focused on conforming to social norms constituting dominant femininity for the purpose of securing a romantic heterosexual relationship. Bridget's incessant quest for heterosexual romance diverts attention from other dimensions of her life which she consciously chose to improve such as her career. Similar to the Disney movies analyzed, Bridget becomes yet another woman who defines herself primarily through romantic heterosexual relationships.

Gender in Bridget Jones's Diary

In spite of Bridget's firm commitment to heterosexual romance, she does not form a subordinate relationship with either Daniel Cleaver or Mark Darcy and thus does not practice a hegemonic form of femininity. Daniel Cleaver embodies many elements associated with dominant masculinity such as handsomeness, heterosexuality, and professional success and concomitantly represents hegemonic masculinity in the sense that he forms hierarchical relationships with other men and women. This was most apparent when he dated Bridget on the premise of monogamy but was secretly involved with another woman and thus exhibited complete disregard for Bridget's feelings. Nevertheless, Bridget does not passively submit to his sexual infidelity but immediately ends the relationship. As Bridget does not form an accommodating, subordinate relationship with Cleaver, she cannot be seen as an embodying hegemonic femininity.

In contrast to Daniel Cleaver, Mark Darcy embodies some elements of dominant masculinity; however, he does not establish and maintain hierarchical relationships with other men and women and thus does not represent

hegemonic masculinity. Darcy may lack Cleaver's good looks and self-confidence but nonetheless he is professionally successful and heterosexually monogamous. Although somewhat arrogant and classist at the onset of the film,
he eventually forms an equal relationship with Bridget that is built upon mutual trust and sexual fidelity.

Although Bridget embodies neither a dominant nor hegemonic form of
femininity, her bodily obsession and self-consciousness illustrate how dominant forms of femininity serve as archetypes for women to measure themselves against. Although dominant femininities are the most celebrated and
therefore most powerful femininities, they diverge from hegemonic femininities in that they do not form an accommodating, compliant relationship with
hegemonic masculinity. Nevertheless, Bridget Jones illustrates how the desire
to embody a dominant form of femininity can prompt women to engage in
unhealthy gender practices and therefore dominant femininities often maintain the status quo.

Sex and the City

The television series *Sex and the City* focuses on the lives of four single professional White women who live in New York City during the late 1990s and
2000s as they embark on a quest for heterosexual romantic love. As the title
suggests, sexuality is a major part of the series, so the series can be commended
for representing women's sexual desires. Nevertheless, the characters have
strikingly different ideas about love, heterosexual relationships, and sexuality.

Carrie Bradshaw is a sex columnist and the series protagonist. In spite of
Carrie's career, close female friendships, and apparent self-confidence, she is
deeply committed to finding Mr. Right. Through Carrie's column, the show
confronts various issues facing modern heterosexual women such as "family
versus career, female self-presentation, motherhood, difficulties in female
friendships, and what sort of compromises are necessary in heterosexual relationships" (Gill 2007, 241).

Miranda Hobbes is a professionally ambitious lawyer who, notably, is not
single-mindedly devoted to the quest for true love. In contrast to both Carrie
and Charlotte, dating and romantic relationships are not the core of Miranda's existence, and she adopts a much more realistic and cynical view of romance. Miranda embodies a pervasive dilemma where career oriented
women who are seeking romantic relationships pose a threat to men and
thus their professional success decreases their value on the heterosexual market. As succinctly surmised by renowned sociologist Michael Kimmel (2008),
"for men, success confirms masculinity; for women success disconfirms
femininity—it's seen as more of a tradeoff. To be taken seriously as a com-

petent individual means minimizing, or even avoiding altogether, the trappings of femininity" (251–52).

Charlotte York is initially an art gallery manager; however, she eventually quits her job after she gets married. Of the four characters, Charlotte is the most committed to the notion of romance and true love and the most sexually conservative. Nonetheless, at times Charlotte makes uncharacteristic remarks which accurately depict the contradiction between modern women's purported freedom to express sexual desire and social norms which stigmatize women for exercising that freedom.

Samantha Jones runs a successful public relations firm and possesses the most nonconventional view of sexual relationships. Samantha claims to have sex like a man, which means short-term, uncommitted, nonmonogamous sexual encounters. Samantha is a self-proclaimed *trysexual*, meaning she is open to an array of sexual encounters. Samantha is firmly opposed to the idea of committed romantic relationships, love, and marriage, although she does have a couple of long-term monogamous relationships. Samantha embodies many characteristics atypically associated with dominant femininity such as unrestrained self-confidence, permissive sexuality, and a commitment to permanent singlehood.

In what follows, I discuss representations of single women in *SATC* by analyzing specific episodes from the series. A pervasive theme in the series is the quest for romantic love, so Carrie, Charlotte, and sometimes even sarcastic Miranda search for romantic love and thus attempt to move out of the single-woman category. Despite this overarching theme, the series also confronts many of the social stigmas attached to single women, professionally successful women, and sexually assertive women. Accordingly, the series also highlights and problemetizes predominant social attitudes toward single women, and thus challenges the heteronormative assumption that women and men necessarily exist in pairs, thereby providing positive representations of single women. I next analyze specific episodes from *SATC* in terms of four prevalent themes: physical appearance, heteronormative sexuality, alternative depictions of family, and representations of single women.

Physical Appearance

In this book, I have continually foregrounded the importance of physical appearance in the construction of dominant femininity. *SATC* also scrutinizes cultural norms which associate women with unrealistic standards of physical perfection. On the one hand, Carrie, Miranda, Charlotte, and Samantha are constructed as young, thin, able-bodied, and thus exemplify culturally idealized standards of beauty and physical perfection. On the other hand, the series also confronts the problematic aspects of this cultural norm by showing the harmful effects of physically damaging bodily maintenance practices. In this way, the series both subverts and reaffirms the salience of appearance in the construction of dominant femininities.

SATC represents physical perfection as a goal women strive to achieve, which can have detrimental health effects. For example, the theme of "Models and Mortals" (Season 1:2) is *modelizers*, or men who exclusively date models. Over the course of the episode, Carrie discusses how contemporary U.S. culture promotes unrealistic standards of beauty and overemphasizes women's appearance. Although Samantha, Carrie, Miranda, and Charlotte are professionally successful, they are represented as threatened by anorexic-like, shallow supermodels whom men apparently prefer to date. Through this episode we see how some men privilege appearance before character and sometimes how professional credentials can decrease women's value on the heterosexual market.

In subsequent episodes, we see the detrimental consequences of striving for physical perfection. In "Freak Show" (Season 2:3) Samantha gets liposuction and a chemical peel and Carrie ponders the notion of aging gracefully. After undergoing plastic surgery, the surgeon discusses with Samantha various other cosmetic procedures; which demonstrate how the construction of heterosexual femininity is an ongoing project that requires continual self-monitoring, maintenance, and renewal. Finally, in "Plus One Is the Luckiest Number" (Season 5:5) Samantha's chemical peel goes awry, causing her to attend Carrie's book launch wearing a veil. Samantha proclaims that women should not be embarrassed about having plastic surgery because it is almost a social mandate. As Akass and McCabe (2004, 191) remark, "This may well be true. But the fact remains that while society may demand perfection it does not tolerate seeing what it takes to attain that ideal" (191). Thus, we see how certain feminine practices should be kept in private and only the finished product publicly displayed.

Samantha, in particular, embodies the struggle many women face who attempt to conform to standards of physical beauty but are subsequently stigmatized when cosmetic procedures go awry. The same could be said of other embodied social actions associated with dominant forms of femininity such as bikini waxes, makeup use, and dieting. Problematically, women are stigmatized as unfeminine when they fail to successfully engage in these social practices while the social norms remain intact. In notable contrast, *SATC* does not blame women who fail to practice aspects of dominant femininity but instead questions the legitimacy of these social practices. Therefore, the series challenges a norm which privileges women's physical appearance and contributes to undermining the salience of appearance as a definitive feature of dominant femininities.

Heteronormative Sexuality

Heteronormative sexuality is a second prevalent theme in *SATC*. Heteronormative sexuality emerges as the normalization of heterosexuality and stigmatization of embodied male femininity. "Boy, Girl, Boy, Girl" (Season 3:4) initially appears to subvert hegemonic heterosexuality through a discussion of bisexuality. In this episode, Carrie's boyfriend, Shawn, casually includes a man in his list of previous relationships. Although Carrie is visibly shocked by and uncomfortable with this revelation, she attempts to remain open-minded and they continue dating. Nevertheless, Carrie remains preoccupied with his bisexuality and continually brings up the matter. Shawn notably challenges heteronormativity when he maintains that a person's character and not gender is most important in a romantic relationship but heterosexuality is renormalized when Carrie ends the relationship. In this episode, *SATC* contributes to reconstituting heteronormative representations of sexuality and not representing diverse sexualities as unmarked.

"Evolution" (Season 2:11) initially appears to challenge a dichotomous view of masculinity and femininity by suggesting that men and women have evolved to the point of possessing masculine and feminine characteristics. Charlotte's boyfriend, Stefan, a sensitive pastry chef with great taste in fashion and interior design, represents an evolved, hybrid form of masculinity. In spite of Stefan's *gay qualities*, Miranda, Carrie, and Samantha confirm that he is a *gay straight man* or heterosexual man with many great gay qualities. Charlotte gradually becomes accustomed to Stefan's gay characteristics and enjoys his cooking, interest in fashion and interior design, and devotion to her. They also have amazing sex which apparently confirms his heterosexuality. Nonetheless, conventional notions of masculinity and femininity are reconfirmed when Charlotte and Stefan are both squeamish over a mouse that is caught in a mousetrap. The episode ends with a shaken Stefan standing on top of a chair and Charlotte looking at him in shock. Apparently, Charlotte's notions of masculinity have not evolved to encompass effeminate men.

Arguably, the show's stigmatized representation of bisexuality and embodied male femininity reestablish the heterosexual matrix and heterosexual desire as organizing principles of gender and the foundation of the unequal relationship between hegemonic masculinity and hegemonic femininity. Bisexuality destabilizes the heterosexuality/homosexuality binary system and threatens to dismantle the heterosexual matrix and disparate relationship constituting hegemonic masculinity and hegemonic femininity. Although bisexuality emerges as a theme in *SATC*, the normative gender and sexuality order is reestablished at the end of "Boy, Girl, Boy, Girl" when Carrie draws an analogy between Alice from *Alice's Adventures in Wonderland* and her own fall into "confused sexual orientation land." Shawn is not only an unsuitable marriage partner but also undatable, as Carrie is clearly uncomfortable with his ambiguous sexuality and ends the relationship.

Embodied male femininity also threatens to contaminate the heterosexual matrix and troubles the hierarchical relationship between hegemonic masculinity and hegemonic femininity. Like Carrie, Charlotte attempts to remain unprejudiced about her effeminate boyfriend; however, once he demonstrates his fear of mice, she realizes that her own notions of masculinity have not evolved to incorporate gay straight men and thus she reestablishes the desirability of macho men. As Henry (2004, 81–82) states, "Although the episode opens up the possibility for a discussion of gender roles beyond the binary masculinity and femininity, it ultimately asserts that *Sex and the City*'s women prefer their straight men on the butch side of the gender scale." *SATC* could have utilized this episode as an opportunity to challenge a rigid binarization of masculinity and femininity. Instead, the episode disseminates conventionalized gender representations which reinstate the norm.

Subverting Heteronormative Conceptualizations of Family

In contrast to strikingly rigid portrayals of masculinity and femininity, *SATC* offers a unique and expanded conceptualization of family, which effectively challenges the normalization of nuclear families. Carrie, Charlotte, Miranda, and Samantha are not portrayed as having close ties with their biological families; however, they compensate for this absence by forming a quasi-family. For example, the girls look for their friends' approval of their boyfriends, seek advice prior to making major life decisions, and provide support and solace during emotionally troubling times. Their behavior parallels that of members of nuclear or extended families, and their homosocial family remains important even once they marry or enter committed romantic relationships. *SATC*'s normalized portrayal of a nontraditional family potentially transforms heteronormative notions of family.

The show's celebration of female friendships is readily apparent in "The Agony and the 'Ex'-tacy" (Season 4:1) where the girls consider the existence of soulmates. Over the course of the episode, the four women question the centrality of marriage and long-term nonplatonic relationships in their lives. At one point Carrie proclaims that married people envy the unmarried, but later she expresses insecurity about being thirty-five and alone. At the end of the episode, Charlotte, who recently separated from her husband, makes a comment that nicely captures the importance and centrality of friendship to their lives by suggesting that they could be each others' soulmates. This reaffirmation of the importance of female friendships over romantic heterosexual relationships challenges heteronormativity by redefining the concept of soul-mates as platonic homosocial relationships.

In "Coulda, Woulda, Shoulda" (Season 4:11), an unmarried Miranda finds out that she is unexpectedly pregnant, and the episode focuses on her decision regarding the baby. Simultaneously, Charlotte is coming to grips with the reality that she is reproductively challenged and is most likely unable to conceive naturally. Miranda's ambivalence toward the prospect of motherhood and Charlotte's desperation to become a mother places a strain on their relationship. Although Miranda decides to raise the baby without marrying the father, Steve, she is clearly not a single mother in the traditional sense. Indeed, the last scene of the episode depicts the three friends gathered around Miranda and offering their support and encouragement.

One final episode which depicts the girls' family-like relationship is "Ring a Ding Ding" (Season 4:6). This episode follows Carrie's heartwrenching breakup with her boyfriend Aidan Shaw. In an earlier episode, Carrie faced eviction from her apartment because the building was going co-op. Aidan proposed that he buy the apartment and they live together. Now that the relationship has ended and Aidan has moved out, Carrie faces a quandary over her future living arrangements. Aidan offers to resell Carrie her apartment; however, she lacks the funds to make the down payment. Carrie first goes to her previous boyfriend Mr. Big to get advice on how to earn the money. Big gives her a check to cover the considerable deposit but Carrie eventually decides to decline. At the end of the episode, Charlotte offers Carrie her engagement ring to use for the deposit. In a sense, the ring symbolizes Carrie and Charlotte's emotional bond, which parallels or even supersedes that of a typical married couple. Carrie's rejection of Mr. Big's offer and Charlotte's symbolic gesture challenges a heteronormative assumption that men financially support women and that strong emotional ties exist only between married couples.

Representations of Single Women

Finally, a fourth and perhaps overarching theme of the series is diverse representations of single women. Similar to the other themes, *SATC* both challenges cultural norms which stigmatize unmarried women by providing alternative representations of single women and reaffirms heteronormative cultural assumptions which associate women with long-term heterosexual partnerships. McCabe and Akass (2004, 13) optimistically argue that "while the women in *Sex and the City* are still attracted to patriarchal stories of happy ever after and fairy-tale romance, women talking about sex, creating humor and sharing laughter are changing the script." I agree that a series which challenges traditional norms constituting dominant femininities can potentially transform those norms. Nonetheless, we still need to critically scrutinize media representations of women which initially appear to subvert but ultimately reaffirm dominant forms of femininity.

Reynolds (2008, 13) has proposed that not only is heterosexuality compulsory but so are long-term partnerships. In "Bay of Married Pigs" (Season 1:3) compulsory coupledom is reflected when Miranda's colleague assumes that she is a lesbian because she is single and sets her up with another woman, Sid, at the firm's annual softball game. Miranda explains the situation to Sid and they decide to participate in the game anyway. At the end of the game, a senior partner, who is attempting to expand his social circle to encompass a lesbian couple, invites Miranda and Sid to dinner. Viewing the invitation as an important networking opportunity, Miranda accepts the invitation. Carrie's voiceover conveys the episode's theme that single people are viewed as aberrant in a couple-oriented society, and thus it may be easier to be part of a couple than remain single. Although heterosexuality may be compulsory, the episode reflects how it is more socially acceptable to be part of a heterosexual or homosexual couple than remain single.

"They Shoot Single People, Don't They?" (Season 2:4) is another episode which questions the legitimacy of a single lifestyle. This episode deals with the theme of whether it is better to fake happiness with someone else rather than remain single. The girls maintain that they are single and fabulous but ironically within a week they all enter relationships. The tension between being single or in a relationship is further exemplified by an article which is supposed to celebrate the fabulousness of a single lifestyle and feature Carrie. Unintentionally, Carrie arrives at the photo shoot for the article late and is photographed looking tired and hungover. When the magazine goes to press Carrie is dismayed to learn that in the *single and fabulous?* heading a question mark has replaced an exclamation point. The episode ends with Carrie choosing to dine alone, which suggests that it is better to be single and happy than in an unhappy relationship. In spite of offering an ending which questions the necessity of being in a romantic relationship, it is worth noting that the four women spend the majority of their time and energy searching for Mr. Right (Gill 2007, 242). While the show does celebrate aspects of a single lifestyle, social norms apparently continue to exert an influence on unequivocally positive media portrayals of a single lifestyle.

The series also confronts the urban myth that women want to be rescued by men. In "Where There's Smoke" (Season 3:1), the girls venture to Staten Island to attend a party sponsored by the New York City Fire Department. Samantha later has sex with a firefighter, which prompts Miranda to ask why firemen are always so attractive, and Charlotte suggests that it is because women desire to be rescued. Charlotte's comment prompts an internal monologue where Carrie invokes but notably provides an alternative ending to the traditional Snow White narrative. In Carrie's version, Prince Charming never materializes, so Snow White wakes up, gets a job, and has a baby through artificial insemination. I concur with Stillion Southard (2008, 156), who maintains that Carrie provides a subversive ending to the traditional Snow White narrative. At the same time, however, Carrie's invocation of this rescue narrative indicates that it remains a pervasive ideological force in contemporary U.S. society. By initially articulating and then offering an unconventional ending to the narrative, *SATC* can be seen as challenging a heteronormative assumption that men protect women.

SATC challenges the social stigma toward single women by constructing hypothetical situations where single women might face others' criticism or judgment. For instance, Miranda faces scrutiny from her realtor and lawyer when she attempts to purchase her own apartment in "Four Women and a Funeral" (Season 2:5). The stigma toward single women is further exemplified when Miranda notices that her mortgage company has mistakenly identified her as separated and she writes them a letter explaining that she is single. This episode notably challenges a heteronormative assumption that women are financially and emotionally dependent on men. In "My Motherboard, My Self" (Season 4:8), at Miranda's mother's funeral, her sister and brother-in-law want her to walk down the aisle together with them. Miranda sardonically comments that a thirty-five-year-old single woman would be more tragic than a coffin. Miranda's comment captures how single women are particularly vulnerable to public scrutiny during certain social occasions. On numerous occasions, Miranda resists and even subverts elements of dominant femininity and accordingly can be seen as an oppositional femininity representation.

The narrative closure offered by the writers of *SATC* is that while there are positive aspects of a single lifestyle, women's ultimate happiness and fulfillment exists within long-term heterosexual partnerships. In "Change of a Dress" (Season 4:15), Carrie raises the legitimate question about whether women really want marriage, babies, and a home, or are just programmed to want these things. Nevertheless, the four protagonists are all in secure, long-term heterosexual relationships by the end of the series. Samantha is the only character who remains faithful to her original mantra that a lifestyle of permanent singlehood and casual sex is more desirable than being in a monogamous romantic relationship. Five years after the series concluded, a movie featuring the same characters was released; at the end of this film, Samantha decides to end her long-term monogamous relationship because she prefers permanent singlehood. Samantha's resistance to compulsory coupledom troubles the relationship between hegemonic masculinity and hegemonic femininity and therefore she can be seen as representing an oppositional femininity.

Samantha Jones: Dominant Oppositional Femininity

Samantha Jones can be seen as a dominant oppositional femininity because she embodies many elements of dominant femininity, yet she concomitantly opposes the hierarchical and complementary relationship definitive of hegemonic masculinity and hegemonic femininity.

First, Samantha works hard to maintain her toned body and physical appearance, which are prime signifiers of dominant femininity. Notably, however, Samantha's femininity is not simply on display for men, thus making her the object of a male gaze. Rather, she uses her embodied heterofemininity to aggressively pursue short-term, nonmonogamous heterosexual relationships. Through her embodied gender practices, Samantha engages with the permissive discourse and challenges the asymmetrical relationship definitive of hegemonic masculinity and hegemonic femininity where gendered norms sanction female but condone male promiscuity.

Second, Samantha's professional success and assertive demeanor challenge a cultural norm which conflates ambition and self-confidence with masculinity. In "Belles of the Balls" (Season 4:10), Samantha meets with hotel tycoon Richard Wright to discuss becoming his public relations agent. Wright refuses to hire Jones after learning that she slept with his architect. Samantha, undeterred, tells Richard that if she were a man, he would have shaken her hand and given her a key to a corner office. Samantha storms out of his office but later receives a call informing her that Richard was impressed by her balls and wants to hire her. This episode portrays Samantha as not only professionally competent and goal-driven but also as unthreatened by adversity.

Third, Samantha's sexuality represents her most explicit rejection of dominant femininity and refusal to complement hegemonic masculinity in a relationship of subordination. In one episode, Carrie describes Samantha as a hybrid because she is a woman with a man's ego and thus engages in uncommitted heterosexual encounters. As discussed, she rejects monogamy and the entire concept of relationships and instead engages in short-term affairs and various *perverse* sexual acts. There are a number of interrelated ways that Samantha subverts a heteronormative gender order where female sexuality is passive and male sexuality active. Samantha illustrates that both women and men can take up a permissive sexuality discourse; however, Samantha is occasionally stigmatized for her gender deviance and thus we also see how women can face social scrutiny and denigration for failing to do gender normatively.

In addition to being open to a wide range of heterosexual experiences, Samantha also dabbles in lesbian sex. For a brief time, Samantha is in a monogamous relationship with Maria. Notably, Samantha sees lesbian as merely a label, which fails to describe the depth of their relationship. Samantha emphasizes Maria's great qualities when she describes their relationship to her friends, which challenges the undisputed normalized status of heterosexuality. Samantha eventually ends the relationship because she finds the level of emotional intimacy which Maria demands exhausting. Samantha remains committed to her original narrative which disavows intimate relationships and challenges the notion that women are inherently relationship-oriented and monogamous.

Samantha also subverts several aspects of heteronormative sexuality by dating a younger man, Smith Jerrod. First, it is common to see older men and younger women couples on the silver screen, but the reverse case is much rarer. Second, Smith is portrayed as more relationship-oriented and Samantha as interested in casual sex. On numerous occasions, Samantha attempts to confine their relationship to casual sex; however, Smith is depicted as desiring a committed monogamous relationship. For instance, Smith attempts to become emotionally closer to Samantha by telling her that he is a recovering alcoholic but Samantha appears uninterested. Although Samantha continually resists viewing her and Smith as a couple, she eventually breaks one of her key principles and they form a monogamous relationship. In many ways, Samantha takes the *masculine* and Smith *feminine* role in their relationship, thereby challenging and potentially destabilizing the heterosexual matrix.

Samantha's embodiment of oppositional femininity is reaccentuated at the end of *Sex and the City: The Movie*. For a time, Samantha is increasingly feminized and appears to embody elements of dominant femininity such as heterosexual monogamy. At the end of the television series, for example, Samantha uncharacteristically tells Smith that he is the most important man she has ever been with. For Samantha, this comment is equivalent to saying "I love you." In spite of this momentary digression, her status as dominant oppositional femininity is reemphasized in the movie when Samantha and Smith are living in California for the sake of his acting career. Although Samantha has professional success, material wealth, and a committed romantic relationship, she appears unhappy and frequently visits her friends in New York. At the conclusion of the film, Samantha ends her five-year relationship with Smith. Samantha explains that while she loves him, she loves herself more and that is the relationship she needs to continue to develop. Clearly, Samantha's explanation subverts the norms of altruism and selflessness, which are typically associated with hegemonic femininity. In sum, Samantha simultaneously embodies some elements of dominant femininity but notably rejects the feminine practices of sexual passivity and humility and thereby challenges the asymmetrical relationship constituting hegemonic masculinity and hegemonic femininity.

Miranda Hobbes: Dominant Oppositional Femininity

Miranda Hobbes simultaneously embodies elements of dominant femininity such as attention to appearance but notably resists the unequal relationship between hegemonic masculinity and hegemonic femininity and thus can be seen as a dominant oppositional femininity.

Miranda is not quite as successful as Samantha in sculpting a thin, toned body, but she does spend time exercising in an attempt to embody this ideal. Unlike Samantha, however, Miranda apparently shapes her body for health reasons rather than for the purpose of actively pursuing heterosexual relationships. Importantly, Miranda subverts the norm that women should modify their bodies in order to increase their heterosexual desirability.

Miranda's physical demeanor also simultaneously conforms to and resists aspects of dominant femininity but in notably different ways than Samantha's demeanor. Miranda's fashion can be characterized as "a conventional rendition of the post-women's movement career woman" (Bruzzi and Church Gibson 2004, 122). The show frequently shows Miranda in dark business suits which downplay her femininity but emphasize her professional authority. At the same time, her use of makeup and stylish hairstyle are characteristics associated with dominant femininities. In contrast to Samantha, whose professional dress emphasizes her femininity through revealing necklines and jewelry, Miranda adopts a more gender-neutral professional demeanor.

Miranda's self-confidence and professional success are other components of her character which subvert normative femininity. Miranda nicely demonstrates how professional success can disadvantage women on the heterosexual market. In "The Caste System" (Season 2:10), for instance, Miranda asks her boyfriend Steve to accompany her to a work function, and they go shopping for a suit. When Miranda attempts to purchase the suit for Steve, he declines because he does not want to view her as a maternal figure. The suit becomes the catalyst which results in Steve claiming that Mirada needs a boyfriend who is on her same level, and he ends the relationship. Miranda comments that she is being punished for her success, which exemplifies the threat professionally successful women can pose to men. "Don't Ask, Don't Tell" (Season 3:12) also addresses this theme when Miranda joins a dating service that introduces her to several potential candidates in an hour. After Miranda introduces herself as a Harvard-educated lawyer, each potential candidate immediately loses interest. Finally, Miranda devises an alternative strategy where she introduces herself as an airline *stewardess*, and she easily gets a date. Miranda attributes her inability to get a date as a lawyer to men's inherent fear of powerful, professionally successful women. Crucially, this episode problematizes the notion that men prefer to possess greater financial power than their partners in nonplatonic heterosexual relationships, and, similarly, how professional success threatens masculine power and thereby disadvantages women seeking nonplatonic heterosexual relationships. Although Miranda does not embody a predatory sexuality like Samantha, nonetheless this discussion has illustrated how her professional success and self-confidence reduce her value on the heterosexual market due to the threat she poses to many men and hegemonic masculinity.

In spite or perhaps because of Miranda's subversive qualities, her character is gradually feminized as the series progresses. Miranda changes from a single, childless career professional inhabiting a Manhattan apartment to a married working mother living in a Brooklyn townhouse. "An American Girl in Paris (Part Deux)" (Season 6:20) particularly demonstrates the feminization of Miranda's character. Steve's mother, Mary, whose memory is somewhat impaired by a stroke, moves in with Steve and Miranda. One day Mary leaves the house unannounced, which sends Miranda on a frantic search for her. Miranda eventually finds a disoriented Mary eating a slice of pizza out of a garbage can. Miranda brings Mary home and is shown giving her a bath while the housekeeper, Magda, watches with an approving smile. After Mary is cleaned up, Miranda asks Magda not to disclose the incident to Steve because it might upset him. In this scene, the emotionally resolute Miranda is juxtaposed by a more maternal, caregiving persona.

Miranda's relationship with femininity is somewhat ambiguous by the end of the series. Some of her definitive characteristics such as chronic workaholism and absence of caretaking ability are eventually softened, which feminizes her character. Nevertheless, when Steve confesses to an infidelity in *Sex and the City: The Movie*, she immediately proclaims that the relationship is over and moves out. Miranda's reaction counters the stereotypical feminine response of crying and emphasizes her emotional resolve. In spite of momentary ruptures in Miranda's character which reflect her femininity, I still maintain that she can be conceptualized as a dominant oppositional femininity.

Oppositional Femininities' Role in Troubling Gender Relations

Samantha and Miranda can be conceptualized as dominant oppositional femininities because they simultaneously practice elements of dominant femininities but contest the unequal relationship between masculinity and femininity. However, as I have continuously indicated throughout this book, a distinction needs to be maintained between oppositional femininities which transgress hegemonic femininity and potentially transform a repressive gender order from those that subvert hegemonic femininity but merely reaffirm the legitimacy of social practices associated with hegemonic masculinity and thus sustain its ascendancy.

Both Samantha and Miranda disrupt power relations through their financial and professional success. *SATC* portrays Miranda and Samantha as assertive career professionals who are unfazed by adversary or conflict and compete on equal footing with their male colleagues. Their power appears to stem from conforming to masculine norms which define professional success, and therefore they are not challenging the exalted status of masculine norms but strengthening the association between masculinity and professional success.

Miranda and Steve challenge production relations by practicing an equal division of domestic labor and childcare duties, which is supported by the assistance of a childcare provider. Miranda and Steve both attempt to juggle the competing demands of work and domestic responsibilities. Steve is a self-employed bar owner who has a more flexible schedule than Miranda, so he can take care of their son, Brady, during the day while Miranda cares for him in the evenings. At the beginning of their marriage, they lived in Miranda's small Manhattan apartment, which was closer to Miranda's workplace but not conducive to family life. Miranda and Steve both adjusted to a longer commute in order to provide their son with a house and backyard. Together Miranda and Steve challenge the hegemony of the male career ideology and heteronormative assumption that domestic work is women's sole burden.

Samantha and Miranda contest emotional relations by performing the required masculine emotional labor of their professions. In *SATC*, self-confidence and assertiveness are requisite forms of emotional labor for the business and legal professions. As previously discussed, in "Belles of the Balls," Samantha is not intimidated by Richard Wright but instead confronts him when he refuses to hire her. Consequently, Samantha is hired for exhibiting self-confidence and aggression. Miranda is also frequently portrayed as non-emotional, competitive, and professionally ambitious, which are stereotypically masculine characteristics. My discussion of the workplace indicated that normative forms of emotional labor are heavily dependent upon workplace norms. Nevertheless, if masculine forms of emotional labor are normative in Samantha and Miranda's respective workplace contexts, then they are conforming to workplace norms and contributing to de-gendering leadership styles.

Samantha's assertive sexuality challenges heteronormativity which constructs female sexuality as conservative, passive, and monogamous. Samantha directly confronts the virgin/whore dichotomy by proclaiming her commitment to nonmonogamous perverse sexual experiences. The portrayal of Samantha as a sexually confident, committed singleton who is unashamed of her single status challenges the canonical image of a lonely spinster and heteronormative assumption that women necessarily find fulfillment through nonplatonic heterosexual relationships. Samantha's assertive sexuality threatens to disassemble the heterosexual matrix and challenges hegemonic masculinity by contesting the assumption that permissive sexuality is men's exclusive possession.

The embodied social actions of Miranda and Samantha challenge symbolic relations by de-gendering masculine social actions and reducing the gap between hegemonic masculinity and hegemonic femininity. The self-confident, goal-driven Miranda, who successfully balances domestic and nondomestic responsibilities, challenges the public/private and masculine/feminine binaries. Samantha also challenges symbolic relations by constructing a professional identity which incorporates elements of both masculinity and femininity and engaging with the permissive sexuality discourse. Both characters' gender practices can be seen as subverting elements of hegemonic femininity and contributing to transforming patriarchal gender relations.

Oppositional femininities such as Samantha and Miranda can function as catalysts for crisis tendencies which transform a patriarchal gender order where hegemonic masculinity is superior to hegemonic femininity. As a professionally successful lawyer and business professional, Miranda and Samantha infringe on men's territory, which contributes to the formation of crisis tendencies in power and production relations. Regarding emotional relations, Samantha and Miranda support the formation of crisis tendencies in two interrelated ways. First, they demonstrate that women are able to perform the requisite emotional labor in their respective professions and thereby contributing to de-gendering these professions. Second, Samantha's unabashedly permissive trysexuality disassembles the heterosexual matrix by challenging compulsory heterosexual coupledom and essentialist social norm that women are inherently relationship-oriented and uninterested in casual sexual encounters. Finally, they promulgate crisis tendencies in symbolic relations by blurring the distinction between masculine and feminine embodied social actions which ultimately transforms norms constituting hegemonic masculinity and hegemonic femininity.

Discussion

Sex and the City and *Bridget Jones's Diary* disseminate contradictory representations of single women which both satirize and in some ways reaffirm the stigma toward single women. Despite celebrating aspects of single life, excluding Samantha, the characters eventually enter committed heterosexual relationships. This narrative closure suggests that while single women may no longer be severely stigmatized, singlehood is still viewed as an ephemeral state that women pass through prior to marriage. The larger implication of this provisional conclusion is that the media contributes to disseminating heteronormative representations of women and men in long-term heterosexual relationships.

This discussion suggests that the heterosexual matrix is still the structuring agent for fictionalized representations of gender and that an incomplete woman discourse continues to influence normative conceptualizations of heterofemininity. This phenomenon was strikingly evident in the Disney films analyzed and more implicit in *BJD* and *SATC*. Due to Disney's status as a cultural icon, children grow up surrounded by these gender representations, which undoubtedly exert an influence on their conceptualizations of gender. The lasting influence of Disney films potentially results in the current situation where many women avidly consume the romance narratives espoused by *BJD*, *SATC*, and other media texts.

The contradictory representations of single women in *BJD* and *SATC* demonstrate how media can juxtapose progressive and retrogressive gendered images, which ultimately reinstate heteronormativity and maintain the status quo. The dominant message espoused by these media texts is that despite women's successes and accomplishments, they are portrayed as somehow unfulfilled or incomplete without heterosexual love. Thus, the complex representations of single women in *SATC* and *BJD* indicate that singlehood is a transitional phase which can extend into one's thirties. Women who prioritize their careers and thus postpone marriage and childbirth may lose the opportunity and ultimately be driven to the point of madness like Alex in *Fatal Attraction*, thus singleness has a limited shelf life for women. Although feminism has provided modern women with many opportunities and a degree of gender equality, the dominant narrative espoused by these media texts is that heterosexual monogamy is still the sine qua non of dominant femininity and outliers who subvert this norm are marked as gender deviant.

Conclusion

In the beginning of the chapter I argued that the media not only represents but also constructs dominant, subordinate, hegemonic, and oppositional forms of masculinity and femininity at the regional level, which can influence viewer's embodied social actions. Simultaneously, however, viewers are not simply passive vessels, but possess agency to accept, contest, or reformulate syndicated images of masculinity and femininity. While we cannot deny that media programs construct and disseminate notions of masculinities and femininities, viewers actively engage with these images in multifarious ways. Due to the media's potential role in constructing gender, critical analysis of gendered media representations is a fruitful endeavor.

In the second part of the chapter I conducted an empirical analysis of representations of masculinities and femininities in *The Little Mermaid*,

Beauty and the Beast, Pocahontas, Mulan, Fatal Attraction, Bridget Jones's Diary, and *Sex and the City.* An incomplete woman discourse was a common theme which permeated these films; however, the salience of the discourse varied according to media text. On the whole, the Disney films tended to disseminate very traditional narratives of physically attractive, sexually conservative, not overconfident women who are fulfilled through empowering a male character and marriage. Reflecting a pervasive gendered ideology of complementary oppositions, the heroines constructed their femininity through empowering male characters, who constructed their masculinity through leading roles and personal accomplishments. Chapters 3 and 4 also detailed how dominant and hegemonic forms of femininity are often associated with performing unrecognized, albeit essential, supportive work.

My analysis of *Fatal Attraction* provided insight into a post-feminist-era media representation of a subordinate oppositional femininity. In sharp contrast to *BJD* and *SATC,* Alex Forrest clearly represented a denigrated oppositional femininity whose failure to follow a normative life cycle characterized by marriage and motherhood resulted in obsession, violence, and ultimately mental illness. The message promoted by this film is that professionally successful single women threaten the stability of nuclear families.

BJD and *SATC,* on the other hand, disseminated more complex representations of femininity which concomitantly reified and subverted dominant femininities. I analyzed each narrative in terms of the prevalent themes of physical appearance, challenging and expanding heteronormative conceptualizations of family, and representing single women. A notable finding was that *BJD* and *SATC* celebrated singlehood only as a temporary state, so the main characters were committed to the quest for and ultimately fulfilled by long-term heterosexual relationships.

The chapter also presented two case studies of gender nonconforming dominant oppositional femininities. Samantha and Miranda's self-confidence, assertive demeanor, professional success, and financial wealth challenged the heteronormative assumption that business and law are masculinized professions and that women are financially dependent on men. Miranda notably embodied a pervasive dilemma where professional success disadvantages women on the heterosexual market. Furthermore, Samatha's nonmonogamous, perverse sexuality subverted dominant notions of heterosexual femininity and demonstrated that women can also engage with a permissive sexuality discourse. Samantha and Miranda indicate that *SATC* also presents images of nonhegemonic, oppositional femininities; however, their transgressive behavior exists firmly outside the confines of hegemonic femininity, so in many ways they reaffirm the normalcy of hegemonic femininity.

The implications of the media analysis are that the heterosexual matrix appears to operate as the structuring agent for heteronormative gender relations in film and television media. *BJD* and *SATC* exist in a post-feminist era where women are supposedly guaranteed a multitude of choices. Disturbingly, however, these media texts disseminate images of modern women who despite their success and various accomplishments still desire and are completed by heterosexual romance. Significantly, heterosexuality and compulsory couple-dom appear to exert an influence on notions of dominant and hegemonic femininities.

6

Conclusion: Femininities
in a Post-feminist Era

This book has focused on the construction of dominant, hegemonic, sub-ordinate, and oppositional femininities within the key social institutions of school, work, and the media. I have continually emphasized throughout the book how femininities are fluid, contextually dependent, and historically situated. Therefore, I provisionally identified a svelte, youthful body, passive heterosexuality, and muted self-confidence as characteristics constituting white, middle-class dominant femininity. These characteristics are contingent, non-static, and situated in a specific time and place.

Masculinity and femininity are located within the symbolic realm of gender relations. Therefore, it is both a mistake and oversimplification to assume that the symbolic realm directly influences material practices such as an unequal distribution of social power and wealth. Nonetheless, masculinity and femininity can and are mobilized to rationalize a fundamentally unequal gender order (Messerschmidt 2010, 6, 158; forthcoming, 26–27; Schippers 2007, 100). I would next like to expand upon my earlier point regarding how embodying hegemonic femininity, which involves forming a complementary and subordinate relationship with hegemonic masculinity, can be women's paradoxical privilege because the same gender practices which constitute hegemonic femininity collectively undermine and disempower women. In the process of forming this relationship with hegemonic masculinity, women serve as handmaidens to the ascendance of hegemonic masculinity and contribute to their own subordination.

An overarching and recurrent theme throughout this book is that the heterosexual matrix is the structuring agent of the gender order in contemporary U.S.

society. The matrix ensures that there are two stable sex categories (male and female) which correspond with two distinct genders (masculine and feminine). Heterosexuality, and I would argue compulsory coupledom, is the magnetic force which purportedly fuses men and women together as complementary opposites, materializing as couples. As Schippers (2007, 90) convincingly argues, however, masculine and feminine are not simply different and complementary but polarized and hierarchical. Consequently, practicing hegemonic masculinity empowers men while performing hegemonic femininity disempowers women. The heterosexual matrix also disempowers individuals with ambiguous gendered identities such as bisexuals and transgendered individuals.

In this book I have also discussed how the heterosexual matrix and heteronormativity are not confined to but extend beyond the realm of sexuality and infiltrate other key arenas of gender relations, which I next consider. I will next discuss how rigid, dichotomized notions of masculinity and femininity support men's monopolization of power and women's subordination in the gender regimes of key social institutions.

In reference to the gender regimes of schools, heterosexual desirability still appears to be adolescent girls' primary source of investable capital in the heterosexual market. Clearly this directs attention from girls' personal ambitions, accomplishments, and abilities, which are undoubtedly more important and boys' main source of investable capital. Crucially, embodying both dominant and hegemonic forms of femininity involves downplaying personal abilities, emphasizing heterosexual desirability, and seeking male validation, which disempower women.

Second, schools do not award feminine activities an equivalent level of institutional prestige recognition as masculine activities. Although girls' and boys' sports have a firm presence in secondary schools, they receive disparate levels of institutional recognition. For instance, boys' sports are sanctioned through schoolwide pep rallies, star athletes are publicly recognized, and the quintessentially masculine sport of football is at the center of homecoming weekend. In contrast, cheerleaders are relegated to the sidelines at these events and cheerleading still struggles for recognition as a sport. Although Title IX may guarantee girls and women the right to equal athletic participation, schools arguably play a role in supporting the ascendance of hegemonic masculinity through sanctioning certain quintessentially masculine sports. The fundamental disparity concerning the value attached to certain activities exemplifies how static, reductionist notions of masculinity and femininity can be strategically constructed and manipulated to rationalize an unequal gender order where women occupy subordinate and men powerful positions.

Regarding the gender regimes of workplaces, the gendering of emotional labor also exemplifies the asymmetrical relationship definitive of hegemonic masculinity and hegemonic femininity and demonstrates how femininity can be used to account for an unequal gender order. Importantly, specific forms of masculine and feminine emotional labor correspond with certain professions which are unequally valued. Thus, masculine forms of emotional labor are supposedly privileged in the nontraditional occupations which I discussed. Drawing on the insightful work of Janet Holmes (2006), I also demonstrated that a rigid distinction between masculine and feminine is not only oversimplistic and reductionist but also can be seen as another strategy to render femininity subordinate to masculinity. Problematically, women can be viewed as naturally suited for feminine professions and specializations and attention can be diverted from examining discriminatory employment practices which discourage women from entering more socially prestigious and better-paid masculine professions. Of course, other factors also impact women's decisions to enter these professions, such as their family-friendliness, which again relates to the gendered ideology that women are children's primary caregivers.

The double bind facing many women professionals is another example of how femininity can serve as a resource to undermine women's success. As I discussed, a fundamental congruence between masculinity and professional success enables men to unproblematically construct their professional identities. Women, on the other hand, face a fundamental incompatibility between their gender and professional identities and therefore risk being assessed as unfeminine when constructing their professional identities. Women who employ a more feminine leadership style may be construed by others as ineffective leaders while those who perform a more masculine or hybrid leadership style risk gender assessment and potential marginalization. Notably, men who enact more feminine, transformational leadership styles are rendered effective leaders. Again we see how femininity can be strategically invoked to undermine professional women by emphasizing their purported unsuitability for positions with institutional authority.

Gendered media representations also provide insight into how femininity is rendered subordinate to masculinity and thus demonstrates the paradoxical nature of embodying hegemonic femininity. Compulsory heterosexual coupledom was a predominant theme in the media texts analyzed; however, the theme had different implications for male and female characters. In the Disney films, an incomplete woman discourse circulated throughout the films; however, there was a noticeable absence of an equivalent incomplete man discourse. The significant implication of this discursive absence is that men's accomplishments outside the heterosexual market override the importance of forming romantic heterosexual relationships. Disturbingly, the heroines' accomplishments were undermined by portraying marriage as their greatest and most important accomplishment.

The women in *BJD* and *SATC* were also rendered somewhat incomplete until they entered long-term heterosexual relationships. Although both media texts positively represented aspects of single life, the dominant storyline was that singlehood is a temporary state and that marriage and motherhood are still part of a normative life trajectory. Even in these contemporary, ostensibly progressive media texts, there was a discursive absence of an unequivocally positive representation of *eligible* single women. Disturbingly, these texts conveyed the message that in spite of the women characters' independence, careers, and intimate same-sex friendships, they were somehow unfulfilled until they found Mr. Right. Reynolds (2008, 50) makes the related point that since marriage and family life are still viewed as women's primary occupation, media representations of single professional women can undermine their noteworthy accomplishments by constructing them as incomplete without male partners. It seems that no matter how much women accomplish, the ability to capture and keep a man's heart is still a cornerstone feature of femininity. Significantly, men hold a great degree of power in the heterosexual market because they judge women's market value and ultimately whether they embody hegemonic femininity.

Oppositional Femininities and a Politics of Resistance

Chapter 1 discussed how individuals do gender in diverse ways; however, those who fail to properly accomplish gender can face gender assessment and sometimes social marginalization. Oppositional femininities exemplify individuals whose sex category and gendered social actions misalign. By refusing to occupy a subordinate position in relation to hegemonic masculinity, these women challenge a dichotomized view of gender and the ascendance of hegemonic masculinity, and thus may offer women a politics of resistance.

Let us now consider those oppositional femininities that do not simply contribute to reaffirming toxic masculine practices, but rather contribute to potentially equalizing asymmetrical gender relations—that is, equality femininities (Messerschmidt 2010, 161).

Women working in nontraditional occupations, who employ diverse strategies to resolve the double bind, can be seen as contributing to transforming an asymmetrical gender order. Although some token women unquestionably appropriated masculine forms of emotional labor, many women employed a range of diverse strategies in order to resolve the double bind. In addition, women's mere presence in stereotypically masculine professions can contribute to ameliorating the association between masculinity and these occupations and thus de-gendering them.

Professionally successful women also contribute to equalizing gender relations by de-gendering the association between masculinity and professional success. *SATC*'s Miranda Hobbes embodied a pervasive dilemma where professional success decreases women's value on the heterosexual market. This is arguably rooted in men's fear of competing with women on equal terms and resistance toward relinquishing control of positions with institutional authority. Oppositional femininities that challenge men's monopolization of powerful institutional positions can contribute to redistributing social power and material resources and equalizing the current gender order.

Single women challenge the basis of a heteronormative assumption that men and women exist as couples. Unfortunately, the media analyzed did not sanction singlehood as a positive lifestyle choice, but instead portrayed it as a temporary state women move through on the way to marriage. More optimistically, however, the fact that *BJD* and *SATC* positively portrayed aspects of singlehood and problematized social stigmas toward single women can contribute to deconstructing the basis of heteronormativity.

Sexually promiscuous women, such as *SATC*'s Samantha Jones, contribute to challenging the hegemony of a passive female sexuality and compulsory heterosexual coupledom. While Samantha's graphic descriptions of her sexual encounters often shocked the other characters, the series did not stigmatize her actions, which can be viewed as a positive portrayal of a confident, sexually assertive woman. In addition, Samantha's *trysexuality* or openness to a wide range of hetero- and even homosexual practices challenged the basis of heteronormativity. Media representations such as this, which portray women as sexually permissive and question the normalcy of heterosexuality, challenge and potentially subvert hegemonic gender relations. Arguably, if men and women could both mobilize a permissive discourse and heterosexuality was noncompulsory, then heteronormative emotional relations would be dismantled and potentially equalized.

The research presented in this book is limited because I have retained a focus on the construction of white, middle-class dominant, hegemonic, subordinate, and oppositional femininities. As a result, my findings and conclusions are not necessarily extendable to other cultures and social contexts within and outside the United States. However, the results of this research have provided insights into how practicing a form of hegemonic femininity can be disempowering. This phenomenon is arguably magnified in other social and cultural contexts. This research can be seen as a first crucial step in shedding light on how embodying hegemonic femininity can be disempowering and thus seen as women's paradoxical privilege. It is the task of further research to empirically investigate how this paradoxical privilege plays out in other contexts.

In conclusion, the results of the analysis presented in this book collectively suggest that an assertion we live in a post-feminist age is premature. On the contrary, men appear to benefit from what Connell (2009, 142) terms a *patriarchal dividend* or "the advantage to men as a group from maintaining an unequal gender order," which manifests in the form of material wealth and access to institutional power. Despite this unsettling claim, oppositional femininities may contribute to destabilizing the hierarchical and complementary relationship definitive of hegemonic masculinity and hegemonic femininity and thereby contribute to redistributing the patriarchal dividend. Accordingly, as feminists, we need to possess both critical awareness and vigilance about how gender hegemony insidiously operates through notions of hegemonic femininity which effectively disempower and subordinate women. It is only through critical scrutiny and deconstruction of these debilitating symbolic representations that we can attempt to redistribute the patriarchal dividend and equalize a patriarchal gender order.

Bibliography

Adams, Natalie Guice, and Pamela J. Bettis. *Cheerleader: An American Icon.* New York: Palgrave Macmillan, 2003.

Adams, Natalie, Alison Schmitke, and Amy Franklin. "Tomboys, Dykes, and Girly Girls: Interrogating the Subjectivities of Adolescent Female Athletes." *Women's Studies Quarterly* 33, nos. 1–2 (2005): 17–34.

Akass, Kim, and Janet McCabe. "Ms Parker and the Vicious Circle: Female Narrative and Humor in *Sex and the City*." In *Reading Sex and the City*, edited by Kim Akass and Janet McCabe, 177–98. New York: I.B. Tauris, 2004.

Bagilhole, Barbara. *Women in Non-Traditional Occupations.* New York: Palgrave Macmillan, 2002.

Baker, Paul. *Sexed Texts: Language, Gender and Sexuality.* London: Equinox, 2008.

Bancroft, Tony, and Barry Cook. *Mulan*, Disney, 1998.

Baxter, Judith. *Positioning Gender in Discourse: A Feminist Methodology.* New York: Palgrave Macmillan, 2003.

———. "'Do We Have to Agree with Her?' How High School Girls Negotiate Leadership in Public Contexts." In *Speaking Out: The Female Voice in Public Contexts*, edited by Judith Baxter, 159–78. New York: Palgrave Macmillan, 2006.

———. "Is it all Tough Talking at the Top? A Post-Structuralist Analysis of Constructions of Gendered Speaker Identities of British Business Leaders within Interview Narratives." *Gender and Language* 2(2) (2008): 197–222.

Bettis, Pamela J., and Natalie G. Adams, ed. *Geographies of Girlhood: Identities In-Between.* New York: Routledge, 2009.

Bolin, Anne. "Transcending and Transgendering: Male-to-Female Transsexuals, Dichotomy and Diversity." In *Third Sex, Third Gender: Beyond Sexual Dimorphism in Culture and History*, edited by Gilbert Herdt, 447–86. New York: Zone Books, 1994.

Brown, Lyn Michael. *Girlfighting: Betrayal and Rejection among Girls*. New York: New York University Press, 2003.

Bruzzi, Stella, and Pamela Church Gibson. "'Fashion Is the Fifth Character': Fashion, Costume and Character in *Sex and the City*." In *Reading Sex and the City*, edited by Kim Akass and Janet McCabe, 115–29. New York: I.B. Tauris, 2004.

Bucholtz, M. "Geek the Girl: Language, Femininity, and Female Nerds." In *Gender and Belief Systems: Proceedings of the Fourth Berkeley Women and Language Conference*, edited by Natasha Warner, Jocelyn Ahlers, Leela Bilmes, Monica Oliver, Suzanne Wertheim, and Melina Chen, 119–31. Berkeley: Berkeley Women and Language Group, 1998.

———. "The Whiteness of Nerds: Superstandard English and Racial Markedness." *Journal of Linguistic Anthropology* 11(1) (2001): 84–100.

Burr, Vivian. *Gender and Social Psychology*. New York: Routledge, 1998.

Butler, Judith. *Gender Trouble: Feminism and the Subversion of Identity*. New York: Routledge, 1999.

Cameron, Deborah. *The Myth of Mars and Venus: Do Men and Women Really Speak Different Languages?* Oxford: Oxford University Press, 2007.

Cameron, Deborah, and Don Kulick. "Introduction." In *The Language and Sexuality Reader*, edited by Deborah Cameron and Don Kulick, 1–12. New York: Routledge, 2006.

———. "Heteronorms." In *The Language and Sexuality Reader*, edited by Deborah Cameron and Don Kulick, 165–68. New York: Routledge, 2006.

Clements, Ron, and John Musker. *The Little Mermaid*, Disney, 1989.

Connell, Raewyn W. *Gender and Power*. Cambridge: Polity Press, 1987.

———. *Masculinities*. Cambridge: Polity Press, 1995.

———. *The Men and the Boys*. Cambridge: Polity Press, 2000.

———. *Gender*. Cambridge: Polity Press, 2009.

Connell, Raewyn W., and James W. Messerschmidt. "Hegemonic Masculinity: Rethinking the Concept." *Gender & Society* 19(6) (2005): 829–59.

Connell, Raewyn W., and Julian Wood. "Globalization and Business Masculinities." *Men and Masculinities* 7(4) (2005): 347–64.

Cottrell, William, and David Hand. *Snow White and the Seven Dwarfs*, Disney, 1937.

Demetriou, Demetrakis Z. "Connell's Concept of Hegemonic Masculinity: A Critique." *Theory and Society* 30(3) (2001): 337–61.

Donaldson, Mike. "What Is Hegemonic Masculinity?" *Theory and Society* 22(5) (1993): 643–57.

Dull, Diana, and Candace West. "Accounting for Cosmetic Surgery: The Accomplishment of Gender." In *Doing Gender, Doing Difference: Inequality, Power, and Institutional Change*, edited by Sarah Fenstermaker and Candace West, 119–39. New York: Routledge, 2002.

Eckert, Penelope. "Language and Gender in Adolescence." In *The Handbook of Language and Gender*, edited by Janet Holmes and Miriam Meyerhoff, 381–400. Hoboken, NJ: Wiley-Blackwell, 2005.

Eckert, Penelope, and Sally McConnell-Ginet. "Constructing Meaning, Constructing Selves: Snapshots of Language, Gender, and Class from Belten High." In *Gender*

Articulated: Language and the Socially Constructed Self, edited by Kira Hall and Mary Bucholtz, 469–507. New York: Routledge, 1995.

———. *Language and Gender.* Cambridge: Cambridge University Press, 2003.

Eder, Donna. *School Talk: Gender and Adolescent Culture.* New Brunswick, NJ: Rutgers University Press, 1995.

Faludi, Susan. *Backlash: The Undeclared War against Women.* New York: Three Rivers Press, 1992.

Fenstermaker, Sarah, and Candace West. "'Doing Difference' Revisited: Problems, Prospects, and the Dialogue in Feminist Theory." In *Doing Gender, Doing Difference: Inequality, Power, and Institutional Change,* edited by Sarah Fenstermaker and Candace West, 205–16. New York: Routledge, 2002.

Fletcher, Joyce. *Disappearing Acts: Gender, Power, and Relational Practice.* Cambridge, MA: MIT Press, 1999.

Foucault, Michael. *The Archaeology of Knowledge.* New York: Pantheon, 1972.

———. *Discipline and Punishment: The Birth of the Prison.* New York: Pantheon, 1977.

Gabriel, Mike, and Eric Goldberg. *Pocahontas,* Disney, 1995.

Garfinkel, Harold. *Studies in Ethnomethodology.* Englewood Cliffs, NJ: Prentice Hall, 1967.

Geronimi, Clyde. *Sleeping Beauty,* Disney, 1959.

Geronimi, Clyde, and Wilfred Jackson. *Cinderella,* Disney, 1950.

Gill, Rosalind. *Gender and the Media.* Cambridge: Polity Press, 2007.

Giroux, Henry. *Fugitive Cultures: Race, Violence, and Youth.* New York: Routledge, 1996.

———. *The Mouse that Roared: Disney and the End of Innocence.* Lanham, MD: Rowman & Littlefield, 2010.

Goffman, Erving. *Asylums: Essays on the Social Situation of Mental Patents and Other Inmates.* New York: Anchor Books, 1961.

Gramsci, Antonio. *Selections from Prison Notebooks.* London: Lawrence and Wishart, 1971.

Gray, John. *Men Are from Mars, Women Are from Venus.* New York: Harper Collins, 1992.

Hamilton, Laura, and Elizabeth Armstrong. "Gendered Sexuality in Young Adulthood: Double Binds and Flawed Options." *Gender & Society* 23(5) (2009): 589–616.

Henry, Astrid. "Orgasms and Empowerment: *Sex and the City* and the Third Wave Feminism." In *Reading Sex and the City,* edited by Kim Akass and Janet McCabe, 65–82. New York: I.B. Tauris, 2004.

Hochschild, Arlie. *The Second Shift.* New York: Avon Books, 1989.

———. *The Managed Heart: Commercialization of Human Feeling.* Berkeley: University of California Press, 1983.

Hollway, Wendy. "Gender Differences and the Production of Subjectivity." In *Changing the Subject: Psychology, Social Regulation and Subjectivity,* edited by Julian Henriques, Wendy Hollway, Cathy Urwin, Couze Venn, and Valerie Walkerdine, 227–63. New York: Routledge, 1984.

Holmes, Janet. *Gendered Talk at Work.* Malden, MA: Blackwell, 2006.

Kendall, Shari. "Framing Authority: Gender, Face, and Mitigation at a Radio Network." *Discourse and Society* 15(1) (2004): 55–79.

Kimmel, Michael. "Saving the Males: The Sociological Implications of the Virginia Military Institute and the Citadel." *Gender & Society* 14(4) (2000): 494–516.

———. *Manhood in America: A Cultural History.* New York: Oxford University Press, 2006.

———. *Guyland: The Perilous World Where Boys Become Men.* New York: HarperCollins, 2008.

King, Michael Patrick. *Sex and the City*, HBO Home Video, 1998–2004, DVD.

———. *Sex and the City: The Movie*, HBO Films, 2008, DVD.

Koller, Veronika. "Business Women and War Metaphors: 'Possessive, Jealous, and Pugnacious?'" *Journal of Sociolinguistics* 8(1) (2004): 3–22.

Krane, Vikki. "We Can Be Athletic and Feminine, But Do We Want To? Challenging Hegemonic Femininity in Women's Sport." *Quest* 53 (2001): 115–33.

———. "Gender Dynamics in Sport Psychology." In *Group Dynamics in Exercise and Sports Psychology: Contemporary Themes*, edited by Mark Beauchamp and Mark Eys, 159–76. New York: Routledge, 2008.

Lamb, Sharon, and Lyn Mikel Brown. *Packaging Girlhood: Rescuing Girls from Marketers' Schemes.* New York: St. Martin's Press, 2006.

Litosseliti, Lia. *Gender and Language: Theory and Practice.* New York: Hodder and Arnold, 2006.

Lorber, Judith. *Paradoxes of Gender.* New Haven, CT: Yale University Press, 1994.

Lusher, Dean, and Garry Robins. "Hegemonic and Other Masculinities in Local Social Contexts." *Men and Masculinities* 11(4) (2009): 387–423.

Lyne, Adrian. *Fatal Attraction*, Paramount Pictures, 1987.

Maguire, Sharon. *Bridget Jones's Diary*, Miramax Films, 2001.

Martin, Patricia Yancey. "'Mobilizing Masculinities': Women's Experiences of Men at Work." *Organization* 8(4) (2001): 587–618.

Martin, Susan Ehrlich, and Nancy C. Jurik. *Doing Justice, Doing Gender: Women in Legal and Criminal Justice Occupations.* Thousand Oaks, CA: Sage, 2007.

McCabe, Janet, and Kim Akass. "Welcome to the Age of Un-Innocence." In *Reading Sex and the City*, edited by Kim Akass and Janet McCabe, 1–14. New York: I.B. Tauris, 2004.

McElhinny, Bonnie. "Challenging Hegemonic Masculinities: Female and Male Police Officers Handling Domestic Violence." In *Gender Articulated: Language and the Socially Constructed Self*, edited by Kira Hall and Mary Bucholtz, 217–43. New York: Routledge, 1995.

Mendes, Sam. *American Beauty*, Dreamworks, 1999.

Merten, Don E. "Burnout as Cheerleader: The Cultural Basis for Prestige and Privilege in Junior High School." *Anthropology & Education* 27(1) (1996): 51–70.

———. "The Meaning of Meanness: Popularity, Competition, and Conflict among Junior High School Girls." *Sociology of Education* 70(1) (1997): 175–91.

Messerschmidt, James W. *Nine Lives: Adolescent Masculinities, the Body, and Violence.* Boulder, CO: Westview Press, 2000.

———. *Flesh and Blood: Adolescent Gender Diversity and Violence.* Lanham, MD: Rowman and Littlefield, 2004.

————. *Hegemonic Masculinities and Camouflaged Politics:Unmasking the Bush Dynasty and Its War against Iraq.* Boulder, CO: Paradigm Publishers, 2010.

————. "The Struggle for Heterofeminine Recognition: Bullying, Embodiment, and Reactive Sexual Offending by Adolescent Girls," forthcoming.

Messner, Michael. *Out of Play: Critical Essays in Gender and Sport.* Albany: State University of New York Press, 2007.

Miller, Jody. *One of the Guys: Girls, Gangs, and Gender.* Oxford: Oxford University Press, 2001.

Pascoe, C. J. *Dude, You're a Fag: Masculinity and Sexuality in High School.* Berkeley: University of California Press, 2007.

Pierce, Jennifer L. *Gender Trials: Emotional Lives in Contemporary Law Firms.* Berkeley: University of California Press, 1995.

Pyke, Karen. "Class-based Masculinities: The Interdependence of Gender, Class, and Interpersonal Power." *Gender & Society* 10(5) (1996): 527–9.

Reynolds, Jill. *Single Woman: A Discursive Investigation.* New York: Routledge, 2008.

Rich, Adrienne. "Compulsory Heterosexuality and Lesbian Existence." *Signs* 5(4) (1980): 631–60.

Roscoe, William. *Changing Ones: Third and Fourth Genders in Native North America.* New York: St. Martin's Press, 1998.

Schippers, Mimi. "Recovering the Feminine Other: Masculinity, Femininity, and Gender Hegemony." *Theory and Society* 36 (2007): 85–102.

Stillion Southard, Belinda A. "Beyond the Backlash: *Sex and the City* and Three Feminist Struggles." *Communication Quarterly* 56(2) (2008): 149–67.

Stone, Pamela. *Opting Out? Why Women Really Quit Careers and Head Home.* Berkeley: University of California Press, 2008.

Sunderland, Jane. *Gendered Discourses.* New York: Palgrave Macmillan, 2004.

Tannen, Deborah. *You Just Don't Understand: Women and Men in Communication.* New York: Morrow, 1990.

Tolman, Deborah L. *Dilemmas of Desire: Teenage Girls Talk about Sexuality.* Cambridge, MA: Harvard University Press, 2002.

Trousdale, Gary, and Kirk Wise. *Beauty and the Beast,* Disney, 1991.

Wajcman, Judy. *Managing Like a Man: Women and Men in Corporate Management.* University Park, PA: Penn State University Press, 1998.

Walsh, Clare. *Gender and Discourse: Language and Power in Politics, the Church, and Organizations.* New York: Longman, 2001.

Weedon, Chris. *Feminist Practice and Poststructuralist Theory.* Oxford: Blackwell, 1987.

West, Candace, and Sarah Fenstermaker. "Doing Difference." *Gender & Society* 9(1) (1995): 8–37.

West, Candace, and Don Zimmerman. "Doing Gender." *Gender & Society* 1(2) (1987): 125–51.

————. "Accounting for Doing Gender." *Gender & Society* 23(1) (2009): 112–22.

Whelehan, Imelda. *Helen Fielding's Bridget Jones's Diary.* New York: Continuum Press, 2002.

Williams, Christine L. *Gender Differences at Work: Women and Men in Non-traditional Occupations.* Berkeley: University of California Press, 1989.

Williams, Joan. *Unbending Gender: Why Family and Work Conflict and What to Do About It*. New York: Oxford University Press, 2000.

Wolf, Naomi. *The Beauty Myth: How Images of Beauty Are Used Against Women*. New York: HarperCollins, 1991.

Index

About the Author

Justin Charlebois completed his PhD in applied linguistics at Lancaster University, United Kingom. He is currently an assistant professor of communication in the Department of Global Culture and Communication at Aichi Shukutoku University, Japan.